GARDENS ARE FOR LIVING

GARDENS ARE FOR LIVING

DESIGN INSPIRATION
FOR OUTDOOR SPACES

JUDY KAMEON

Principal Photography by Erik Otsea
Foreword by Jonathan Adler
Illustrations by Judy Kameon

RIZZOLI
NEW YORK

New York · Paris · London · Milan

CONTENTS

FOREWORD

Judy Kameon should be a full-time Artist's Muse.

Haven't you always felt that Joni Mitchell was missing a fourth Lady of the Canyon from her feminist counterculture anthem? She needed a chick with a green thumb and a mystical understanding of plants and of how to live a sublimely Californian life. Judy is that chick, the ethereally gorgeous Earth Mother who wears an extremely compelling sunhat.

I wouldn't be surprised if Nancy Meyers's next movie is inspired by Judy. I can imagine the satisfying chick flick about a gorgeous L.A. landscape designer who has it all. After watching the film, contented viewers would have the same conversation they have after every Nancy Meyers joint—they would be scratching their heads as they try to figure out how a gardening girl lives such a fabulously rich and glamorous life. They would be enchanted by this fantasy set in Elysian Park, a story in orange and plywood. And they would be kvelling about that intoxicating garden!

Eat, Pray, Love lady, Elizabeth Gilbert, could have saved herself a lot of time and frequent flier miles if, instead of schlepping around the world, she had just pulled up a chair at Judy's table and gotten schooled in some Oral Herstory. She would have learned that the key to spiritual enlightenment lies in California sunshine. She would have basked in Judy's chic but friendly Elysian Park house, eyed her gorgeous and sweet hubby, and delighted in the antics of their adorable kid. The book would've been called *Garden, Nibble, Sip, Play, Laugh* and it would've been even better.

And if we could magically resurrect them—Monet, Constable, and Van Gogh would be on the next Pan Am flight to LAX. They would hop in a cab and go set up easels in one of Judy's gardens. They would marvel at the poetry of the gardens at the Parker Palm Springs. In Judy, they would see a kindred spirit, someone who can harness the power of color and light to create beauty.

As something of an *artiste* myself, I often think of Judy when making a pot or designing a chair or decorating a home. I think of her special brand of California Modernism, her light but assured touch, her ability to make something seem as if it were just meant to be that way, as if it were always there, as if it had been uncovered rather than created. I know that one of my pieces is good if it would look at home in Judy's pad.

And now you, dear reader, can find your Muse. You can learn from Judy how to make your garden, your yard, your *life* much more sunny, more chic, more optimistic.

Immerse yourself in this book, enter Judy's groovy California world, and feel your chakras tingle. . . .

—Jonathan Adler

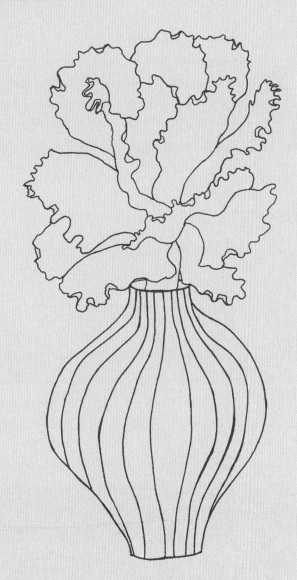

INTRODUCTION

Twenty years ago, while California was experiencing a drought and I was dealing with financial uncertainty, I decided to create a garden. During flusher times, I had purchased the empty lot next to my bungalow in the Elysian Park neighborhood of Los Angeles with the express intention of making a beautiful oasis. As a painter I generally worked late at night, which left plenty of time during the day for other pursuits. Although I had no clue how to begin, working on my garden became my magnificent obsession. In the making of my own garden, and later gardens for many others, I learned a lot about designing landscapes and met a number of kindred spirits who share my passion for all things outdoors.

GROWING UP

I grew up in Santa Monica in the 1960s. At that time Santa Monica was an unpretentious, low-key beach town, where no one locked their doors. I was a lucky kid in many respects. My afternoons were filled with simple pleasures, like drawing classes and walking my dog. Much of the year I woke up to gray, foggy mornings—the marine layer rolling in and floating among the pine trees that lined the streets and surrounded my second-story bedroom.

In the summer, the neighborhood kids ran around with bare feet and we played Kick-the-Can in the street until our mothers called us home for dinner. Some of the most fun we had was in our own backyards. My house was one of the few with a swimming pool and was the epicenter of all warm-weather activity. We would frolic in the pool for hours—playing long games of Marco Polo and King of the Hill—until our fingers resembled pale, bloated prunes and our eyes turned red from the chlorine. My mom was a gracious host, serving us post-pool-time snacks of orange slices and Neapolitan ice-cream sandwiches. To this day, an ice-cream sandwich conjures up my childhood in the most profound way—my equivalent to Proust's madeleine.

My dad wasn't much of a cook. He made soft-boiled eggs for breakfast and salami sandwiches for lunch. He was, however, the king of our Weber BBQ. He would grill steaks, ribs, hamburgers, and chicken—all prepped by my mother, of course. Like a surgeon at the operating table, Dad would man the grill while my brother and I handed him various tools, sauces, and platters at his command.

Now that I have my own family, and Weber grill, and the good fortune to have my own backyard with a pool, I find myself thinking about these moments. And while I don't think they are particularly unique, my memories are important to me and far-reaching. Cooking, eating, playing, and spending time with family, friends, and neighbors are truly meaningful experiences. It is through this kind of social interaction that we create our communities and forge relationships. Now, more than ever, as we live in an increasingly distant and virtual world, there is a greater need and desire to have real experiences, conversation, and contact with other people. There is no better place to do that than in your own backyard.

GOING PRO

My path to becoming a landscape designer was not a straight line, but rather a meandering stroll. It began when I was nineteen and working as a number cruncher for a fashion designer while going to college. Soon after I had started on what I thought was my new career, the designer confided that the fashion business was 99 percent business and 1 percent creative. I quickly made my exit and vowed to become an artist. I had idealistically decided that my life's work would be 100 percent creative, and I set out to make that happen.

I graduated from UCLA with a BA in Fine Arts, which qualified me to do exactly nothing in the job market. At the time there were virtually no outlets for young L.A. designers and artists to show their work. My world was populated with a vast number of creative people in this category, so I thought it would be a good idea to open a store/gallery called Livestock to showcase their talent. With six thousand dollars as seed money (inheritance from my beloved piano teacher, Dena), I rented a space and set up shop. The store was located at the wrong end of Melrose Avenue, on a small street prophetically named Heliotrope (a lovely, sweet-smelling, old-fashioned flower). It was a charming storefront in an old brick building, with cheap rent, and just across the street from the practice space used by the seminal punk band X, one of my all-time favorites. I took this as a good omen.

As the new owner of a forward-looking boutique, I decided to market my young designers with a series of small fashion shows. My strategy worked well enough and soon I was staging events in various downtown nightclubs. At one of these shows, a director friend who was in attendance asked me if I would provide the wardrobe for a music video she was shooting for a young rapper. I was given a budget of three hundred dollars; whatever I didn't spend I could keep. This was a veritable windfall. The video became an MTV hit, and a stylist was born.

I eventually closed my store to focus on painting and supported myself by working for several directors over the next few years, dressing a range of musicians, models, actors, and dancers. But styling proved to be a greater distraction from painting than I had anticipated, so I quit the profession. I started to show my paintings and even found gallery representation, but my fledgling art career was not paying the bills. It was during this time that the empty lot next to my house captured my attention.

MY GARDEN

The only real gardening experience I had was from my childhood, planting tulips for my mother at a nickel a bulb, growing carrots in a raised bed, and collecting cymbidium orchids and African violets. My lack of experience didn't deter me from jumping in once I became focused on creating my own garden. My head was full of images of Sissinghurst, Barrington Court, and Tintinhull—just a few of the many grand and wonderful English gardens I had had the good fortune to visit. It wasn't the vast lawns and multitudes of clipped hedges that spoke to me; rather, it was the gorgeous and colorful ornamental borders full of exotic blooms and intoxicating fragrance that I found completely captivating.

I started my informal design education by devouring innumerable books, haunting nurseries, befriending growers, and cultivating relationships with plant geeks. I experimented madly. My property was on a slope, so I carved up the land into a series of terraced gardens and gave each space a different aesthetic and plant palette. I used a variety of building materials, combining stone, pigmented concrete, wood, and gravel.

The leap from designing my own garden to designing for others was a fairly natural one. It happened when my garden was about five years old and had begun to develop some real character. The tiny trees and shrubs I had planted were now providing shade and privacy, the small plants that survived the rock-hard clay soil had filled out, and the simply furnished patio areas felt friendly and inviting. A dear friend was over and asked if I could help him with the backyard of his new house. I thought, *Sure, why not?* The next thing I knew, every time I went to an art opening, a dinner, or a party, I would invariably meet someone who had just bought a house and needed help with their outdoor space. Things snowballed very quickly, and before I knew it I was designing gardens all over town.

The relationship between me and what once was a patch of dirt and weeds has been profound. Over the years, through observation, trial and error, and teaming up with some accomplished builders and landscape installers, I've soaked up knowledge about hardscape, grading, irrigation, planting, and lighting. I've also found great inspiration from creative friends and their inventive and unexpected uses of outdoor space, ranging from gorgeous plantings to open-air bathing to hillside amphitheaters. In showcasing some of their work as well as my own, I hope to share the same awe and delight I've experienced.

My own garden, now mature, has brought me full circle. I now have my own small family—my husband, Erik, and our son, Ian—with whom I happily share my life and my garden. Ian reminds me of what it was like to be his age and full of wonder and curiosity. Now it is his turn to plant seeds, grow carrots, and pick fruit and flowers. The pleasure I derive from having a noisy Sunday, with our garden full of kids and friends, and a table laden with good food and drink, is immeasurable. My hope is to share that joy and inspire others to join me in creating their own special outdoor places.

INSPIRATION FOR LIFE OUTSIDE

Inspiration can take many forms and come from many places. I will always remember my first bite of arugula at a picnic table set in the English countryside and how I was inspired to grow it at home. The dazzling red ornamental border at Hidcote Manor Garden in Gloucestershire, England, triggered my own chromatic studies when designing plantings. The breathtaking series of gardens full of dramatic combinations of palm trees, succulents, and cacti at the Lotusland estate in Montecito, California, influenced the linked gardens we created for the Parker hotel in Palm Springs. Inspiration is significant and meaningful—it provokes ideas, creates goals, and galvanizes action.

Sometimes inspiration strikes closer to home, while you are doing something as ordinary as sitting in an armchair with a good book. In the earliest days of making my own garden, my favorite book was the *Sunset Western Garden Book*. I read it cover to cover, yearning to absorb everything inside. I wanted my garden to be beautiful and flourish. I didn't want to make amateurish mistakes (although that was inevitable); I hoped to make good and informed choices.

I can't remember a time in my childhood without the presence of *Sunset*'s books and magazines. Their shiny pages were filled with gorgeous images and instructive text that led the way to understanding and embracing modern design and living. It was within these pages that many people first encountered modern landscape architecture and the works of Garrett Eckbo, Thomas Church, James Rose, and Dan Kiley. *Sunset* promoted the rich connection between architecture and landscape and celebrated the concept of outdoor living as a lifestyle. Not only was this modern approach completely appealing and accessible, but it was also made attainable. Frequently included was the work of one standout photographer, Julius Shulman, whose unparalleled and exhaustive documentation of this era of design inspired and touched so many of our lives.

I had the good fortune to meet Julius on a photo shoot. My firm had designed the gardens for a Richard Neutra home in the Pacific Palisades, newly renovated and restored to perfection by a talented architect named John Hughes. Julius had photographed the house when it was first built and had been brought back to shoot its latest incarnation. I had no intention of going to the shoot—I can be shy when meeting people I admire—but the architect called me repeatedly and said I should go. I thought I would quietly slip in the door, watch the maestro at work, and slip out again, but that was not meant to be. The moment I showed up, Julius spotted me and shouted across the room, "Who's that? Come over here!" I was delighted to discover that Julius was completely gregarious and in no time we were chatting away. He loved the garden, which made me swoon with happiness, and said he would like me to come see his own.

Julius's garden was a veritable jungle—a wild and lush hillside dense with jade plants, agaves, and an assortment of trees that he had planted over many years. The original property was fifty acres, most of which he donated to the Santa Monica Mountains Conservancy so that it is now protected as open space. Julius was interested in not just showing how something looked, but in capturing and communicating how people lived in their spaces and illuminating the marriage of architecture and landscape. He was among the first to include people in his architectural photographs and the warmth and style they convey contributes greatly to the impact of his images and our lasting perception of these places. He lived to the age of ninety-eight, working until the very end of his life, always passionate about photographing architecture and landscape and connecting with the people who created them.

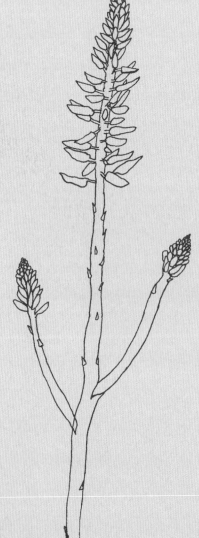

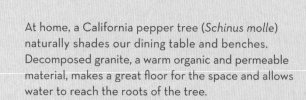

At home, a California pepper tree (*Schinus molle*) naturally shades our dining table and benches. Decomposed granite, a warm organic and permeable material, makes a great floor for the space and allows water to reach the roots of the tree.

above: The main patio at our house sports an eclectic mix of pieces from Plain Air, our line of outdoor furniture. The multicolored concrete pavers that make up the patio were made in batches, using a mixture of concrete and dry pigments to produce a variety of colors, and then laid in random order on a bed of sand. The low stone wall was built to be bench height; for parties, I put out cushions for additional seating.

left: Nestled under the canopy of a fig tree and framed by the bold simplicity of Case Study architect Whitney Smith's modern pergola, picnic-style dining never looked more chic. The boxy geometry of the open grid is the perfect counterpoint to the organic form of the adjacent trees. Long benches replace individual chairs and lend clean lines to the arrangement.

Stylish and fun outdoor living exemplified by the mid-century master James Rose continues to provide a wealth of inspiration. Food, family, and comfortable furniture are still some of the best ways to enjoy your outdoor spaces.

GETTING STARTED

Beginning a landscape project can be a daunting undertaking. Here are some important things to consider before starting so that you can make good choices that work for you.

SPACE PLANNING Every outdoor space, whether small or large, deserves a well-thought-out plan. Start with an overall layout of hardscape (patios, walkways, walls, and stairs) and planting areas. I make sure there is ample room for the furnishings by noting their placement on the layout.

PROGRAM *Program* is an architectural term that refers to the elements you want to include in your project. Are you pining for a fire pit, pool, dining area, or all of the above? I always put together a wish list for each project and go from there.

AESTHETIC Are your tastes more traditional or modern, formal or casual? Think of your garden as an extension of your home; it should be consistent with your interior.

CLIMATE Learn what climate zone you inhabit—knowing this is essential to the success of your garden. The climate zone map is based on the average annual minimum winter temperature and will tell you what plants will thrive in your specific climate.

SOIL Know your native soil type. Clay retains moisture and nutrients but has poor drainage and can be expansive—something to consider when installing stone or concrete and certain kinds of plants. Sandy soil has great drainage and doesn't expand, but it can require more water and organic material, depending on your plant choices.

WATERING How much water you use and the system you use to deliver it are critical aspects of the design. There are a number of ways to water a garden and each has its pros and cons. I prefer drip irrigation for planting areas against the house and narrow spaces, spray irrigation for large planting beds, rotors for big hillsides, and hand-watering for pots.

MAINTENANCE Be realistic about how much or how little care your garden will receive and choose your plants accordingly. Gardens do best with regular maintenance, but there are lots of plants and outdoor materials that require only small amounts of attention.

The Parsons-style table and upholstered benches
provide ample seating for friends and family. The
benches are extra wide for comfort, and are even a
good place for little ones to lie down and take a nap.

above: James Rose, one of the mid-century masters of landscape design, offers a light touch with geometric hardscape design. His graphic composition of oversize concrete pavers and lawn makes a compelling setting for lounging, whether on a cot-like chaise or a few pillows artfully thrown on the grass.

right: Large, cast-in-place concrete pavers lead to a built-in bench, sited for enjoying the adjacent view. The bench invites reading and napping, as well as provides seating for the occasional dinner party. Filling the gaps between the pavers with lawn softens the look of the concrete.

top left: Ralph Stevens's bold use of sculptural succulents for the Tremaine Garden still feels completely modern, fifty years later. His dramatic composition of various succulents and Korean grass (*Zoysia tenuifolia*) shows how much impact can be made with a focused plant palette. *Julius Shulman photography archive, 1962.*

top right: Floating pavers provide a dramatic bridge to a bi-level patio in this stunning Buff, Straub and Hensman–designed residence. The exterior wall can be used for informal seating. A giant cushion on the patio floor, topped with lots of throw pillows, looks comfortable and inviting and really extends the interior of the house to the outside areas. *Edwards house, 1959.*

left: This outstanding *Aloe* 'Hercules' (tree aloe), with its muscular trunk and fleshy foliage, more than lives up to its moniker. Tall, shrubby planting that masked the pool was replaced with a mixture of low succulents and perennials, which open up the space and enhance views within the garden.

Architect and design guru William T. Georgis designed this dramatic pool for his private West Coast getaway. A raised planter ingeniously created planting space at the foot of a large retaining wall, which we filled with statuesque junipers and striped flax. Water spilling from pin jets into the pool is a lovely soundtrack in the already tranquil spot.

top left: Vintage chaises outfitted with snappy striped cushions sit atop a small concrete and hand-laid pebble patio. The icing on the cake is the jumbo-size cocktail umbrella shading the space.

top right: Colorful cushions top French market carts retro-fitted into chaises for poolside lounging. Orange epidendrum, an easygoing variety of orchid beloved by hummingbirds and humans alike, fills big glazed pots.

right: A red banana tree underplanted with lavender evokes memories of travels to some of our clients' favorite places. Timber bamboo layered behind the banana tree provides greater privacy.

opposite: Casual and glamorous poolside entertaining, captured by society photographer Slim Aarons. Stacks of pillows create loads of poolside seating, and the overall flavor is delightful.

top left: A crisp white wall is the perfect backdrop for a grouping of tangerine wall planters. Filled with the succulent *Echeveria* 'Mauna Loa', the planters are watered by hand once a week and have built-in drainage for easy care.

top right: Countless photographs by Julius Shulman have inspired me over the years, and I particularly adore this one of his own wife and daughter, relaxing at home. This sunny portrait perfectly captures the spirit of California living, and the casual arrangement of furniture and planted pots looks completely fresh and inviting. *Shulman house (Los Angeles, Calif.), 1950.*

left: Architectural Pottery, founded in 1950 and based in Los Angeles, made some of the most highly sought-after modern ceramics in history, including my favorite wall-mounted planter by Malcolm Leland. Thankfully, the collection was revived in the late 1990s and its pieces once again grace many of the finest landscapes worldwide.

A bowl of succulents planted as a centerpiece for a dining table was deemed to resemble Esther Williams's swim cap. Small details like pots and planters are often the finishing touches to a landscape.

PUTTING OUT
THE WELCOME MAT

The front garden is like the face of your home and, much like your face, can communicate all kinds of things. A front garden can be open and welcoming, private and mysterious, or something in between. It can be an exterior foyer—an intimate space that you move through quickly—or a gracious courtyard in which you can linger. A front garden should provide enough privacy so that you don't feel on display but without being fortress-like. The home's entrance should be easy to locate. Whichever way you go, the landscape should enhance the experience of arriving home, whether the design is crisp and graphic or more layered and wild. I like to think of front gardens as the first room of your house.

When I was growing up, front gardens were almost always a big swath of green lawn with a meager border of flowers, perhaps a few shrubs, a tree or two, and a simple path. The result was something completely neutral, nonthreatening, and without any real purpose, save for getting to the front door. There certainly wasn't a distinctive voice, style, or point of view expressed, and it was rarely a space to be lived in and enjoyed. The front garden of my childhood home was no exception.

Times have changed. There is a veritable revolution going on when it comes to what people are doing with their front gardens—it is one of the most exciting developments in residential landscape design. The first order of business for most of us is to rethink, resize, or even rip out the lawn. While this idea may seem sacrilegious to some, it may be one of the most responsible and productive things you can do as a landowner. For anyone who lives in dry and arid climates, the lawn is an incredibly thirsty green carpet that does not give as much as it takes. For others, a big front lawn may be a missed opportunity to use your space in a more productive and inspiring way. I love to design a beautiful courtyard entrance, a private patio to inhabit, or bold compositions of plants that weave in herbs, flowers, and foliage for cutting. Now when clients tell me they want to rip out their front lawns, I practically burst into applause, and the design wheels immediately start turning.

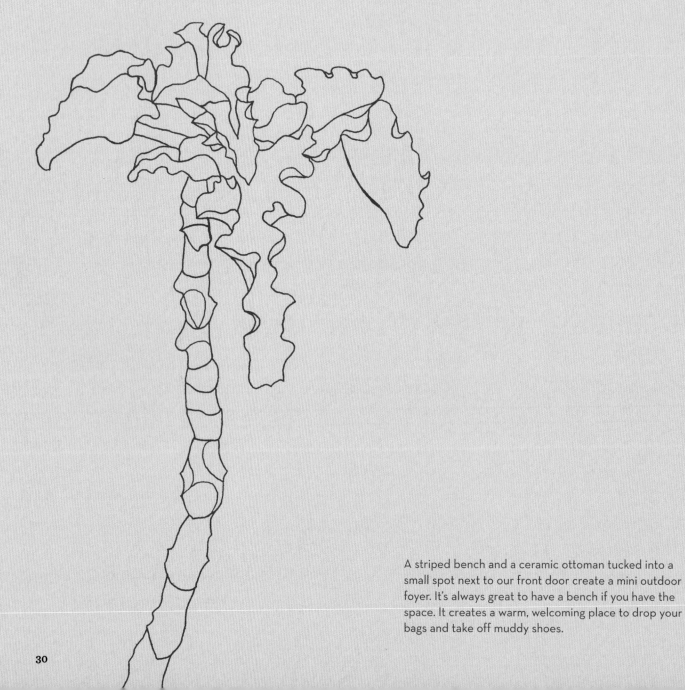

A striped bench and a ceramic ottoman tucked into a small spot next to our front door create a mini outdoor foyer. It's always great to have a bench if you have the space. It creates a warm, welcoming place to drop your bags and take off muddy shoes.

above: Front hillsides pose special challenges. Rather than live with an unimaginative ivy-covered slope, a graphic tapestry garden was planted. The *Acacia baileyana* 'Purpurea' trees at the top of the slope create privacy from the neighbors and a more treehouse-like feeling. At night, the tree canopies are lit, which enhances the evening view from inside looking out.

opposite: A combination of white, black, and silver foliage was inspired by the restrained exterior palette of a mid-century residence. Gray-and-white-striped *Agave americana* 'Mediopicta Alba' punctuate a leafy silver groundcover while black aeoniums and flax (*Aeonium* 'Zwartkop' and *Phormium* 'Black Adder') provide nice hits of dark foliage for dramatic contrast. Gophers are a common problem, so a strategy of peaceful coexistence was adopted by planting everything in chicken wire gopher baskets, which protect the roots of the plants.

left: A luminous steel-and-Plexiglas screen creates a private court-yard entrance replacing an ordinary ficus hedge. The pigmented concrete surface doubles as a play space and parking area. At night, the whole screen is backlit and glows like a big glass box, framed by the canopies of the surrounding trees.

above: A composition of succulents creates a botanical reef-like feeling on dry land. Gravel is used to topdress the flat planting areas, which immediately gives the garden a clean and finished look. The gravel also improves drainage and helps suppress weed growth and retain moisture in the soil, reducing maintenance and water needs.

SIMPLE STRATEGIES FOR AN INVITING SPACE

I think of front gardens as a transition from public to private space. While giant hedges or tall fences provide lots of privacy, they can sometimes seem unfriendly. Conversely, a front lawn that rolls up to the sidewalk can often feel too accessible and exposed, so it's nice to have some kind of delineation between the public space and your home. When possible, I like to strike a balance somewhere in the middle. Here are some tried-and-true strategies to consider when designing a front garden.

KEEP IT SIMPLE Simple schemes and low-maintenance plantings can look good year-round without requiring lots of work. Be sure to include an abundance of evergreen foundation plants and perennials to provide consistent visual structure. Annuals, plants that last a single season, can be used to add color and interest, particularly in cooler climates.

ADD A TREE A tree or two can provide screening for privacy, frame an entrance, and provide important scale. Always consider the mature size when selecting trees to ensure they will grow to a pleasing proportion for your home and property. Small-scale trees are lovely for bungalows and cottages.

CREATE PRIVACY Use a mix of ornamental shrubs to screen out the street and provide delineation from the sidewalk in lieu of a hedge, especially for smaller spaces that don't have the room for a hedge and an ornamental border. This provides visual interest without requiring significant maintenance or financial investment.

CREATE MORE PRIVACY If greater privacy is desired, install hedges only as tall as needed for screening passersby, cars, and neighboring houses, and put in a beautiful gate. If possible, keep a few feet of space in front of the hedge on the street side or by the entry for ornamental planting to balance the height and signal the entrance.

INCLUDE FRAGRANCE Plant something fragrant as a welcoming element. There are few things lovelier than being greeted by a whiff of lavender, citrus blossoms, or the herbal notes of rosemary and sage.

top left: Flanking a front door with a pair of pots or planters is a simple touch for creating an inviting entrance. Sky blue boxes, planted with strappy maroon *Cordyline* 'Red Star', play off the orange walls for a lively graphic composition.

top right: A nondescript open front entrance is made over into a private courtyard oasis. The low planter wall encircling the space retains soil and provides informal seating around the Moroccan-inspired water feature, welcoming family and friends.

right: The front entry at our office includes a few inviting touches, transforming the parking area into a courtyard that can be used for events. A solid wall provides the perfect opportunity to stage a daybed, and a bright yellow door is a cheery signal of where to go.

The dramatic front garden at Balenciaga is a lunar landscape, in keeping with the edgy aesthetic of the French fashion house. Raised planters designed to mimic the display cases inside are filled with succulents rather than the company's highly coveted handbags, accessories, and footwear, and flank a front path made of black lava pavers.

The lower foliage of the timber bamboo has been removed to offer a glimpse into a front atrium at this Neutra-designed residence. Pea gravel is used as a groundcover under the bamboo, which immediately gives it a neat appearance and helps retain moisture in the soil.

Simple stairs made of rough-hewn lumber jog up a front slope, with a slight undulation from side to side, to create an informal entry. Flanked by ornamental grasses, kangaroo paws (*Anigozanthos* 'Red Cross'), and the variety of lavender used in the perfume trade (*Lavandula x intermedia* 'Grosso'), the rustic ascent smells as good as it looks.

top left: A quiet spot in front of a guesthouse has foliage that mirrors the surrounding natural landscape in a canyon setting. The sight lines were carefully considered and plants were specifically chosen to screen out adjacent rooftops and frame the best aspects of the view.

top right: Screening the neighbors is a popular request. Layering shrubs, ornamental grasses, and perennials masks the adjacent houses without closing in the space or creating a hard delineation. The front walkway is an asymmetrical grid of oversize concrete pavers, planted with a ground cover of wooly thyme (*Thymus pseudolanuginosus*), which can take light foot traffic and forms a dense mat of tiny leaves, perfect for using in between pavers or stones.

right: This exuberant composition hits several notes—color, texture, form, and scale. The graphic form of red star dracaena (*Cordyline* 'Red Star') pairs beautifully with the static sculpture of blue foxtail agave (*Agave attenuata* 'Nova') and the softer texture and movement of Mexican feather grass (*Nassella tenuissima*). Some ornamental grasses self seed in certain conditions, like this *Nassella*, so it's best to check before planting to see what works for your site.

above: An edible garden thrives in a sunny spot in a front garden. Tucked behind a dwarf olive hedge, raised beds and a new lemon tree are easily accessed from a gravel path off the front landing.

left: The vibrant planting is a focused palette of silver, bronze, and fresh green foliage with splashes of bright chartreuse.

opposite: A straight row of concrete pavers inset with pebbles is softened by planting with a ground-cover thyme (*Thymus lanuginosus*). The colorful painted front door is a cheery touch that neatly ties into the interior decor and inspired the flower color of the kangaroo paws (*Anigozanthos* 'Orange Cross').

A FRESH APPROACH
TO FRONT GARDENS

There are a myriad of reasons to rethink your front garden. Here are a few to consider:

CURB APPEAL Increase the curb appeal and value of your home by creating something beautiful; it will benefit you financially and emotionally. A gracious entrance is very welcoming for everyone, including yourself.

CAPTURE SPACE Increase usable space by creating a front courtyard or small seating area. It will be like adding a new room to your house.

INSULATE Naturally insulate your house by planting trees to keep interior spaces cooler in the summer and warmer in the winter. In warm climates, plant evergreen varieties for shade year-round. In cooler climates, plant deciduous varieties that drop their leaves in the winter to let in more light.

SAVE WATER In drier climates, use less water by removing lawn and installing plants that require little water.

BECOME PERMEABLE Keep hardscape to a minimum for driveways and walkways and incorporate permeable options, like crushed rock, gravel, decomposed granite, or larger areas of planting, to minimize water draining offsite.

ENHANCE VIEWS Improve the interior views looking out by layering trees, shrubs, and plants. Most of us spend more time inside looking out at our gardens than outside looking in, so they should look beautiful from both vantage points.

BE PRODUCTIVE Grow plants you can eat and flowers you can cut, and spend more time enjoying the outdoors.

A concrete paver walkway leading from the street is softened by the feathery plumes of oriental fountain grass (*Pennisetum orientale*). Stonecrop (*Sedum brevifolium*) is a great succulent ground cover to use between pavers and provides a pleasing touch of green.

above: A romantic hillside garden, made by the artists Laura Cooper and Nick Taggart, includes a colorful outdoor dining area in a front patio. Trees make wonderful natural canopies for dining, providing shade when it's sunny and a structure for hanging lights for the evening, extending your use of the garden from day into night.

right: The orange flowers of a torch aloe (*Aloe arborescens*) provide the sole pop of color in the garden. The balance of the palette is a cool range of blue, silver, gray, and cream that mirrors the colors of the home's interior decor. Feathery plumes of dwarf pampas grass (*Cortaderia selloana* 'Pumila') mimic the lush textiles used throughout the house.

opposite: A small patio used for outdoor breakfasts lets diners enjoy the morning sun. Close to the street, this front garden was easily made private with a combination of shrubs and small trees, which are kept pruned to leave room for ornamental flowers and foliage. Reclaiming much of the space for personal use but still leaving room for a welcoming entry is a modern approach to front-yard design.

left: A tiled front courtyard makes for a compelling entrance to a house built in the 1930s. The pale blue house with white and black trim inspired the choice in tile as well as the plant selection, a subtle palette of blueish greens, silver, and violet.

right: The glossy tiled water feature stars as the centerpiece of the courtyard. A simple cascade of water masks the noise from the street below.

opposite: A cozy seating area features an oval marble coffee table made for the space. The see-through mesh of vintage-style clam chairs is a great visual counterpoint to the generous daybed, creating an inviting entrance.

Blue Flame Agave
Agave 'Blue Flame'

Australian Willow
Geijera parviflora

Blackbird Spurge
Euphorbia 'Blackbird'

Large Purple Aeonium
Aeonium 'Zwartkop'

Good Vibrations Juniper
Juniperus horizontalis 'Hegedus' Gold

New Zealand Flax
Phormium 'Dusky Chief'

Trees, Shrubs, and Plants for Front Gardens

Bloodgood Japanese Maple
Acer palmatum 'Bloodgood'

Carol Aeonium
Aeonium 'Carol'

Cassa Blue Flax Lily
Dianella caerulea 'Cassa Blue'

Variegated Japanese Mock Orange
Pittosporum tobira 'Variegatum'

Wooly Grevillea
Grevillea lanigera 'Coastal Gem'

Vesuvius Coral Bells
Heuchera 'Vesuvius'

There are lots of great evergreen and perennial trees, shrubs, and plants that can be used
to keep your front garden looking beautiful year-round. I try to use varieties that require
relatively little water and maintenance. This is a selection of plants that I use often.

CREATING COMMUNITY SPACES

"The crickets are chatting," Ian whispered in my ear. Indeed they were, a perfect organic accompaniment to the already dulcet sounds of voice, lute, and recorder. My family was attending a concert of obscure baroque composers at Folly Bowl, the exquisitely handcrafted amphitheater created by artists Susanna Dadd and James Griffith. Folly Bowl is both a place and a happening. Not to be confused with the legendary Hollywood Bowl, Folly Bowl has much the same conceit—you bring a picnic and a bottle of wine, and take a seat on one of the terraces. We mingled at intermission, trading oatmeal cookies for freshly picked figs, and marveled at the beauty of the evening. But my most lasting impression was the experience of participating in the event, of being part of the gathering of friends, neighbors, and music lovers. All were brought together in this one magical place by the shared vision of two people, several tons of broken concrete, and a lot of elbow grease.

Community, by its very definition, means a unified body of individuals. I've discovered over time a number of communities of various interests, ages, and sizes, all united in their passion for doing things outdoors. In addition to the community garden, one of the more traditional types of outdoor communities, I have come across the likes of an outdoor book club, community oven, mural project, and architectural laboratory. Each brings together a group of people around a central idea and goal, which becomes quite meaningful in the scheme of the individuals' lives.

One community that I was involved with many years ago was a loose-knit group of artists, educators, and misfits who formed a garden club called The Germinators. Our inspired moniker came from the always hilarious, and sometimes controversial, newsletter written by the talented garden scribe and designer Ivette Soler. We were united in our obsession for all things horticultural, and our monthly nomadic garden parties included much food, drink, and garden geekdom amid the revelry. We swapped plants and recipes, and shared cuttings, seeds, and our own personal experiences in garden making. Our little group made a big splash during the annual garden design competition at the Los Angeles Arboretum, with The Germinators sweeping the awards, including the prize for Best in Show, and garnering the ire of some of the more seasoned professionals we were competing against. *Garden Design* magazine deemed us "The Coolest Garden Club in America." Eventually, with other things occupying more of our attention, like work and family, we found less time for our regular garden-based gatherings. Now, when we do come together, whether at a lecture, an Easter egg hunt, or an art opening, we often find ourselves huddled in a corner talking about plants and gardens.

I have consistently found that garden-centric people want to share what they have as well as what they know, from trading eggs for apples to providing resources for hard-to-find plants and advice on how to compost with worms. Clubs can pop up in different ways. Ours started informally— initially just a small group of friends getting together, and then each of us inviting other like-minded friends. We took turns hosting meetings at our homes, and each gathering included a garden tour and potluck meal, which always kept our get-togethers fun and fresh. Now, with the Internet, clubs can form easily with sites like Meetup, where people with shared interests can find one another and join or start a club. The Los Angeles Bread Bakers, which started with a handful of passionate amateur bakers, now boasts a membership of more than six hundred people, and it continues to grow. I know firsthand that getting involved in a group, club, or community can be a completely enriching and life-changing experience.

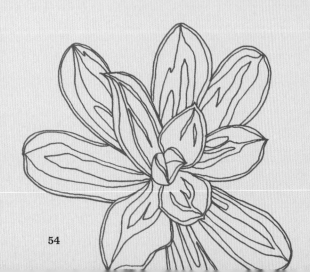

Set in a large growing field that was formerly an acre of asphalt, the outdoor classroom at the Garden School Foundation is used daily for teaching children about the world through hands-on education. The garden was designed by Nancy Goslee Power & Associates.

top left: A vast array of fruits, vegetables, herbs, and flowers are grown year-round, many from seeds that are donated to the program, which is called Seed to Table.

top right: A simple pergola provides shade throughout the day and is decorated with colorful gourds painted by the children.

left: Kids experience the process of planting, tending, harvesting, investigating, cooking, and eating the fruits and vegetables they grow in the program, which is enthusiastically supported by parents, neighbors, and volunteers.

above: A community of parents, led by architect Dana Bauer, team up with students of all ages to create a dynamic and dimensional mural at Citizens of the World Charter School. This ingenious project uses UV-rated materials to transform an existing chain link fence into a giant vertical tapestry that will evolve over time and serve as a prototype for future school projects.

right: The unique design for the mural is based on geologic formations. The pattern was first painted onto the fence and then the children worked in teams to fill in the massive outdoor framework by hand-knotting each strip of cloth.

above and left: Inspired by the tradition of plein-air painting and the flora of Los Angeles, painters Carolyn Castaño and Hadley Holliday invited a large group of artists to make art outdoors at a series of events they dubbed "Garden Party." Artists working in a variety of media—including drawing, painting, and photography—bring their own supplies and set up wherever suits their fancy. Here a gathering takes place in Eika Aoshima and artist Roger Herman's garden, which they designed themselves.

opposite: "Garden Party" gatherings take place in different garden settings, both public and private, and explore the challenge of capturing nature within the context of an artistic social environment. The hosts consider the act of participation equal in importance to the artwork produced.

above: A modest front yard has been transformed into a cultural hotspot for architects who want to experiment with making real, rather than virtual, models. Founders Jenna Didier and Oliver Hess named their influential research center Materials & Applications. The courtyard, which is open to the public, attracts people from all walks of life, eager to experience designs like *Project S'more* by Edmund Ming-Yip Kwong.

opposite: Aptly named *Bloom*, a recent installation by Doris Sung, Ingalill Wahlroos-Ritter, and Matthew Melnyk, comes across as the metallic love child of a dragon and a flower. Thousands of articulated silver scales join in a curvaceous form that swirls skyward, like a flower opening to the sun. The piece renders beautiful dappled light when the sun is high and hot, and creates surprisingly friendly spaces to inhabit.

above: In a vertiginous canyon, the artists Susanna Dadd and James Griffith have painstakingly built Folly Bowl, their ambitious vision for a private outdoor amphitheater. Open-air concerts that continue to grow through word of mouth bring together an appreciative audience of friends, neighbors, and music lovers.

right: Built-in benches are scattered throughout the space, and concert-goers are encouraged to picnic, making for a perfect summer evening.

opposite: Initially motivated by the need to stabilize their hillside property, Susanna and James acquired several tons of broken concrete, first collecting it from the side of the road, then later importing truckloads of the stuff, and began the arduous task of building rows and rows of terraces. Seating varies from patches of grass to rugged built-in benches.

left: For a project in Berkeley, a narrow bit of space along a fence line provided an opportunity to plant a row of colorful small succulents. The wide median between the sidewalk and the street features a variety of plants that are native to California, including canyon prince wild rye (*Elymus condensatus* 'Canyon Prince') and Cleveland sage (*Salvia clevelandii*).

right: The children of the neighborhood enjoy this simple wooden swing, tucked under the canopy of an old loquat tree (*Eriobotrya japonica*).

opposite: A lush streetscape is appreciated by admiring neighbors and passersby. The hundred-foot-long retaining wall that runs the length of the property became an asset rather than a liability with the addition of layered planting and trees.

left: A standout feature of our office is a demonstration garden showcasing favorite plants, materials, and furnishings. The lower patio with built-in seating multitasks as our daily lunch room, occasional conference room, and seating area for special events. A concrete retaining wall doubles as the back to the U-shaped seating area, maximizing the use of the space and giving an up-close garden experience.

right: Unusual plant combinations are a highlight of our demonstration garden. Here, purple-flowering compact indigo spires sage (*Salvia* 'Mystic Spires Blue') vividly contrasts with orange kangaroo paws (*Anigozanthos* 'Orange Cross') and chartreuse golden breath of heaven (*Coleonema pulchellum* 'Sunset Gold').

A roaring fire centers an outdoor salon at the top of our hillside demonstration garden. Long benches ensure an abundance of seating, and landscape lighting extends the party from day into night.

Reedstem Orchid
Epidendrum 'Red'

Metallic Echeveria
Echeveria gibbiflora 'Metallica'

Rock Purslane
Calandrinia grandiflora

Intrigue Canna Lily
Canna 'Intrigue'

Red Yucca
Hesperaloe parviflora

Coppertone Stonecrop
Sedum nussbaumerianum

Plants to Grow and Share

Chocolate Mint Scented Geranium
Pelargonium 'Chocolate Mint'

Black Hens and Chicks
Sempervivum 'Black Mountain'

Siberian Iris
Iris sibirica 'Caesar's Brother'

Canyon Prince Wild Rye
Elymus condensatus 'Canyon Prince'

Showy Stonecrop
Sedum spectabile 'Autumn Joy'

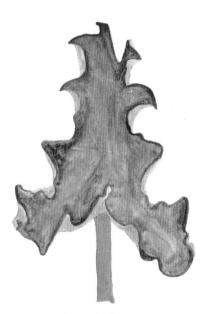

Velvet Elephant Ear
Kalanchoe beharensis

Many of my favorite plants were first introduced and given to me by friends. I like to return the favor and often use cuttings of plants (including written instructions for planting) to decorate gifts or bottles of wine when I'm invited to someone's house. Here are some plants that are really easy to grow from cuttings or divisions and are great to share.

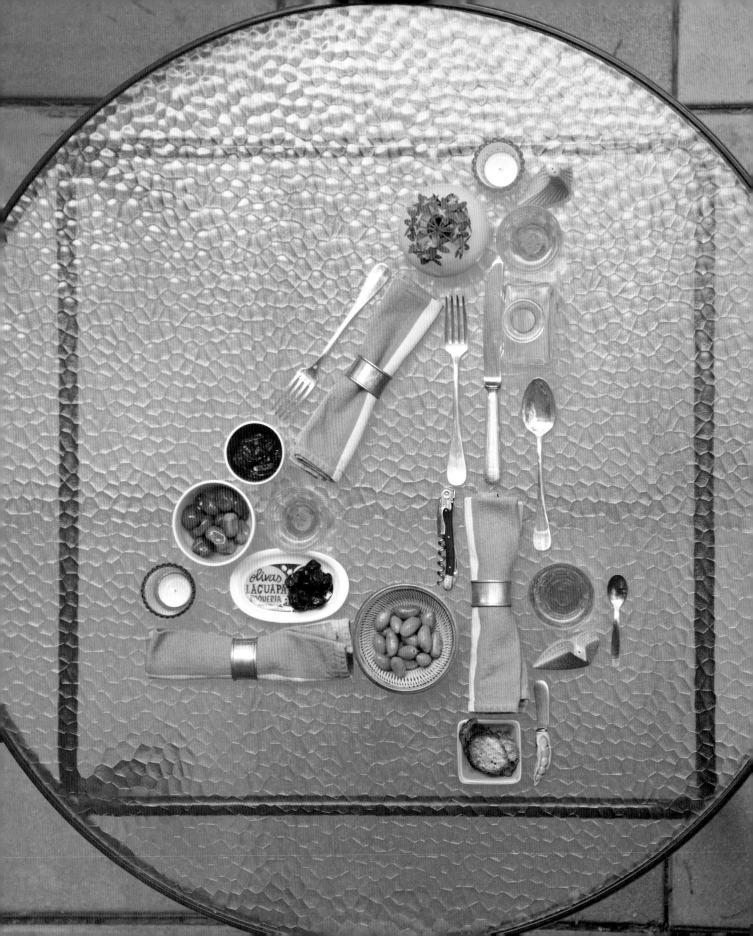

GATHERINGS FOR FRIENDS & FAMILY

Many years ago, when I moved into my tiny bungalow, I realized that the biggest room I had wasn't *in* my house but outside it—my rambling backyard. Not that there was anything in it, except a bunch of weeds and an enormous pepper tree, but I saw the potential. I have always loved entertaining, so my natural impulse was to make a multitude of inviting spaces that could be used for all kinds of gatherings. The first thing I did was create a generous flat area underneath the pepper tree, big enough for a long dining table that could comfortably seat a dozen or more people. Many of our gatherings continue to be in the garden: Sunday lunches, Fourth of July barbecues, springtime birthday celebrations, summer dinners, and all-day hangouts by the pool.

Getting together with friends and family is important and has the capacity to enhance our lives immeasurably. Virtual contact is no substitute. When you add good food, a nice glass of wine, and a comfortable chair in a garden setting, entertaining becomes something truly special. Ranging from playful to romantic, outdoor gatherings have a magic all their own. Outdoor entertaining can be simple—you don't have to be a great cook to do it. Pick up a nice piece of cheese, a loaf of bread, some olives, and a bottle of rosé, or put out nuts and a pitcher of sangria. A small terrace with a few pillows thrown around can work as well as a fully furnished patio. Either way, guests will not want to leave.

Whenever I tackle a new project, I ask my clients a lot of questions and listen closely. Do they like to have small gatherings or big groups, or both? I immediately start thinking about how best to develop the space for outdoor gatherings while making it beautiful. Whether the design is formal or casual, intended for cocktails around a fire pit or picnics on the lawn, the space should work for both daily life and entertaining. My friend Timm had a favorite spot in his backyard to which he would drag a folding chair, sit back, and enjoy the view. We built a huge bench on that very spot, long enough for him to lie across for reading and a nap, and large enough to seat several people side by side. The first party he had after the garden was completed was on Thanksgiving. He brought out a large dining table, plopped it in front of the bench, and set up some chairs; dinner was served.

left: Easy snacks are always appreciated, and there's no need for plates or utensils when fingers will do. Tile-top tables make great outdoor surfaces and hold up well in most climates.

right: I enjoy making colorful bouquets, freshly cut from the garden. For dining, I favor lots of small arrangements that easily work around platters of food and bottles of wine and water and don't block the view of people across the table.

opposite: A nicely set table is always a welcoming touch and part of the fun of getting ready for a party. At our informal gatherings, I often serve family style and let people pass food around and help themselves.

The space underneath a large deck was unused and unloved until wood siding, a twenty-two-foot-long banquette, and a pair of coffee tables were added. A big blue pot with a fulsome Swiss cheese plant (*Monstera deliciosa*) softens a corner and a giant piece of sisal, cut and bound, makes a great floor mat for the lounge.

top left: A large daybed makes it possible to have a long and lazy Sunday with friends—just add food, drink, and the Sunday paper. I got the idea to make a huge daybed after a trip to Bali—now we can vacation at home. A discreetly placed water feature burbles soothingly, adding to the getting-away-from-it-all feeling.

top right: At parties, small side tables are great for small plates or, in this case, serving dessert. If you have more than one seating area in your garden, try moving around to enjoy different parts of the garden. It's fun and more comfortable than sitting in one chair for a whole evening.

right: An assortment of Moroccan lanterns hang like jewelry and help transform the space into an inviting destination. Frosted Plexiglas panels, which let light in but obscure the view of the street, create privacy. At night the panels are backlit, illuminating the whole space with a romantic glow.

above: A custom dining set with ample seating for family and friends was made to fit this nook. The orange tile is a nice pop of color in the leafy treetop setting.

opposite: Hardwood decking and a custom railing transform an ordinary balcony. The railing was mounted to the side rather than through the deck for a cleaner look. Hardwoods like ipe make great long-lived surfaces but do require periodic light sanding and resealing to keep their lustrous dark finish.

left: On a sprawling hillside property, a series of intimate gathering spaces maximize the use and enjoyment of the land. A large retaining wall created enough flat space for a small pool but proved to be a visual eyesore. Densely planted layers in front of the wall make it practically disappear.

above: A secluded seating area for two is a lovely spot for a quiet gathering. The billowing vine planted directly above softens the look of a large retaining wall and a simple steel bowl makes an informal fire pit.

FAVORITE TIPS & TOOLS FOR OUTDOOR ENTERTAINING

GOOD FURNITURE Comfort is essential, so don't skimp when it comes to furnishing your outdoor spaces. Pick pieces that feel as good as they look. If you invest in handsome pieces that are built to last, you won't be sorry.

PILLOWS Keep lots of pillows on hand—they're great for turning low walls and stairs into informal seating for many.

TRAYS These are great for transporting food and drinks from inside to outside, and they help make the post-party cleanup easier.

SELF-SERVICE Use the top of a low wall or a table as a sideboard for drinks or a buffet. People like to help themselves, and it minimizes time spent running in and out of the house.

FOCAL POINT Create seating around a fire pit, a low water feature, or a big coffee table. People will naturally gravitate toward the spot.

CASUAL TABLETOP Use sturdy, reusable tableware that you don't have to worry about damaging—tin and enamel camping plates, stainless flatware, simple glass tumblers, and patterned cotton napkins—rather than paper and plastic.

SHADE For daytime gatherings, entertain underneath the canopy of a tree, a pergola, an awning, or a couple of umbrellas.

FINGER FOOD Serve appetizers that can be eaten by hand, like olives, spiced nuts, wedges of cheese with toasted bread, dates, and radishes.

REFRESHMENTS Put out big pitchers of water, fresh lemonade, or batches of cocktails, and let people fill up. It's always fun to offer a special drink—just make sure there is plenty to go around.

CANDLELIGHT When entertaining at night, light candles in glass votives or hurricane lanterns just before sunset, and place them on tabletops and walls to minimize rushing around in the dark.

WARMTH Pass out throw blankets on chilly evenings to keep your guests cozy and happy.

left: A generous built-in daybed provides gracious seating for many. The wall of the adjacent raised planter doubles as the back of the daybed, providing the perfect setup for a large bolster and colorful pillows.

right: When grapefruit season arrives, part of our harvest is used to make this delicious aperitif *vin de pamplemousse*, or grapefruit wine. A macerated mixture of white wine, vodka, vanilla bean, and lots of fresh grapefruit, lemon, and orange juices, it makes a refreshing cocktail served over crushed ice with a splash of sparkling water and a candied kumquat.

above: A wood pergola painted black shelters a dining area, just the right size for a set that seats six. The retractable striped awning is made of a resilient outdoor fabric and can be easily opened and closed to provide shade or sun. A glazed red pot tucked into the planting makes a discreet water feature.

left: A vintage pair of hanging lamps are retrofitted with low-voltage outdoor wiring and strung up in a tree as part of the landscape lighting.

opposite: A plastered wall makes an instant backdrop for backyard movie screenings. Just add pillows and popcorn for fun summertime entertainment.

above: An awkward corner at the back of the property was too small for chaises but perfect for a wedge-shaped daybed. A green screen of Henkel's yellowwood (*Podocarpus henkelii*) adds another layer of privacy and satisfying lushness.

left: The light profile of the hoop chairs pairs nicely with the graphic silhouette of the tree aloe (*Aloe* 'Medusa'). Casual poolside seating that is lightweight and can be easily moved around offers guests great flexibility.

above: Succulents happily thrive in contained environments like these concrete planters. The board-form concrete wall shows the grain of the wood used in the forming process, creating a lovely organic pattern.

right: A gravel path meanders through a varied planting of ornamental grasses, succulents, and colorful sages and flax (*Salvia* 'Mystic Spires Blue' and *Phormium* 'Red-Dark Green'). The informal path connects the front entry to the back garden so guests can come straight to the pool without going through the house.

left: The wildly patterned encaustic tile floor makes an exciting outdoor surface for a casual seating area in this collaboration between Kismet Tile and Zoe Bios Creative. A freestanding terracotta chiminea keeps people warm when temperatures dip.

right: Charming orange lanterns mimic the ripe fruit hanging from a citrus tree. Overhead lighting offers a nice balance to in-ground lighting and greatly enhances nighttime entertaining.

top: Family meals can be enjoyed at this poolside dining set throughout the year. The table accommodates a large umbrella for sunny days, which can be removed during cooler months.

bottom: In lieu of chaises, built-in seating doubles as a place to gather. Outdoor speakers, masked behind planting, make music readily available.

left: Bright splashes of color echo the palette of the garden. The tones of the furnishings and garden are an extension of the home's interior decor and reinforce the idea of indoor/outdoor living.

right: An existing broken concrete wall was the starting point for developing an inviting seating area. Walls make great backdrops for staging big seating pieces and when combined with tall plants, help create a room-like feeling.

opposite: A narrow back garden with a soaring hillside in a canyon setting was broken up into a series of connected patios. In this space, lush planting wraps a cozy seating area and cool evenings are enjoyed in the warmth of a simple fire pit.

above: The eclectic planting is a combination of succulents and Mediterranean and subtropical perennials. The sculptural forms of foxtail agave (*Agave attenuata*) and mauve echeveria (*Echeveria* 'Afterglow') are complemented by the strappy foliage of Berkeley purple flax (*Phormium* 'Wildwood') and billowing white shrub roses (*Rosa* 'Iceberg').

right: A floating built-in banquette frames a canyon view on a hillside property. Drinks and lanterns fit neatly on built-in side tables and keep the floor space open for circulation. The planting comes right up to the banquette and wraps the back side, screening out neighbors and creating a feeling of enclosure while staying open to the view.

top left: The striking pots of sticks-on-fire (*Euphorbia tirucalli*) add a finishing touch to the poolside seating area. The foliage resembles red coral, but is aptly named—the sap can sometimes burn the skin.

top right: I have cushions made to put out along low walls, creating an abundance of informal seating for parties with little setup. I always include a matching tote bag for easy transportation and storage.

right: Big trays are great for parties. Fill them up, set them down, and soon you'll find them empty.

opposite: This generous banquette was once a low concrete block wall hidden behind a hedge of bamboo. Increasing the height of the wall and hiding speakers in the plantings make it a perfect setting for enjoying cool evenings, accompanied by Frank Sinatra and a dry martini.

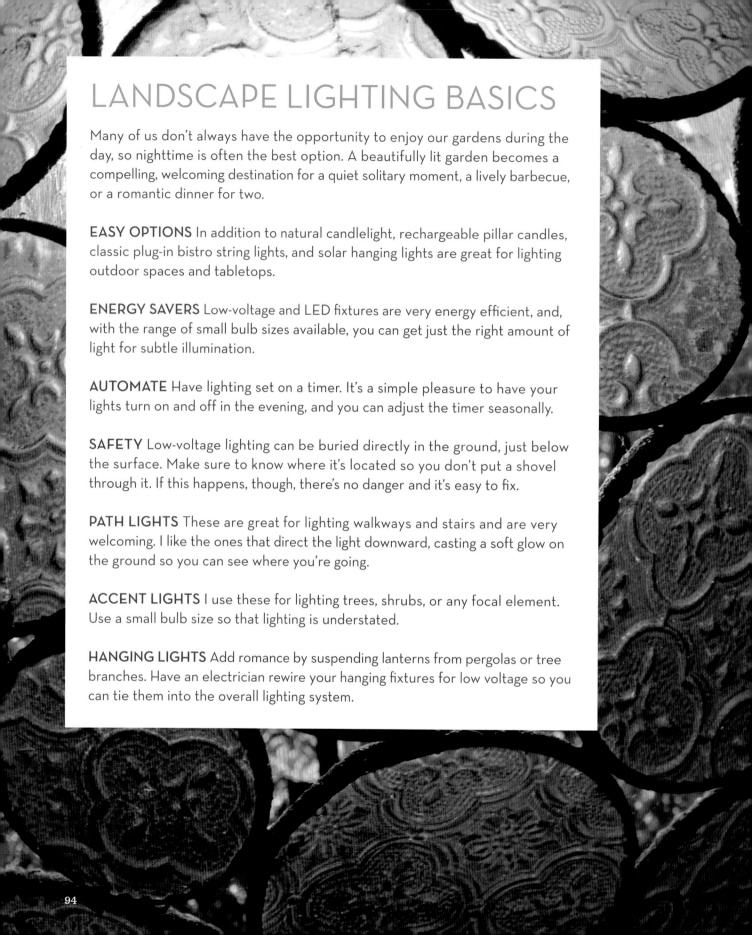

LANDSCAPE LIGHTING BASICS

Many of us don't always have the opportunity to enjoy our gardens during the day, so nighttime is often the best option. A beautifully lit garden becomes a compelling, welcoming destination for a quiet solitary moment, a lively barbecue, or a romantic dinner for two.

EASY OPTIONS In addition to natural candlelight, rechargeable pillar candles, classic plug-in bistro string lights, and solar hanging lights are great for lighting outdoor spaces and tabletops.

ENERGY SAVERS Low-voltage and LED fixtures are very energy efficient, and, with the range of small bulb sizes available, you can get just the right amount of light for subtle illumination.

AUTOMATE Have lighting set on a timer. It's a simple pleasure to have your lights turn on and off in the evening, and you can adjust the timer seasonally.

SAFETY Low-voltage lighting can be buried directly in the ground, just below the surface. Make sure to know where it's located so you don't put a shovel through it. If this happens, though, there's no danger and it's easy to fix.

PATH LIGHTS These are great for lighting walkways and stairs and are very welcoming. I like the ones that direct the light downward, casting a soft glow on the ground so you can see where you're going.

ACCENT LIGHTS I use these for lighting trees, shrubs, or any focal element. Use a small bulb size so that lighting is understated.

HANGING LIGHTS Add romance by suspending lanterns from pergolas or tree branches. Have an electrician rewire your hanging fixtures for low voltage so you can tie them into the overall lighting system.

Glamorous poolside dining wouldn't be complete without a chandelier. Low-voltage lighting throughout the garden enhances the overall nighttime experience and looks as beautiful from inside the house as from out.

HOMEGROWN FOOD & FLOWERS

My first vegetable garden was a gift. When I was six years old, my parents had a wood box made and filled it with good soil. Tucked between my playhouse and the pool in our backyard, next to the roses, it was a raised bed of my own. I excitedly opened colorful seed packets and carefully sowed the tiny seeds, and like the little boy in my favorite childhood book, *The Carrot Seed*, watered, weeded, and waited for my modest crops to come in. When harvesttime came, the results were not exactly stellar, but I still marveled at the entire process.

This sense of wonder and delight has stayed with me over the years. When I moved into my little bungalow with the weed-filled backyard, one of the first projects I tackled was planting some fruit trees and a variety of vegetables and herbs. It's a lot of work to grow your own food—it requires a real commitment of time, energy, and space, often with mixed results, aesthetic imperfection, and the occasional sunburn. That being said, it is lovely to step into the garden and pick a bunch of lemons for lemonade or some fresh sprigs of thyme for stuffing inside a roast chicken.

There are innumerable benefits to growing your own food and flowers. The taste and fragrance alone are worth the effort. There is profound gratification in making a salad from freshly clipped arugula, serving a bowl of creamy homegrown lima beans, or making a flower arrangement from your own blooms. Working in the garden provides a momentary break from our hectic lives and connects us to our place, our seasons, and our food. We can also ensure that our food and flowers are being grown with sustainable methods. Simple actions, like composting with kitchen scraps and garden clippings, can be deeply rewarding. My own family enjoys releasing ladybugs in the spring, as well as hatching praying mantis eggs and then setting the tiny creatures free in the garden.

More and more people I know are taking domestic production a step further: growing flowers for market, keeping bees for honey, and raising chickens for eggs. For the most part, like myself, they are self-taught and have learned through trial and error. As one friend said, "Always a student, never a teacher." Working with nature is a humbling experience in many ways, which is not necessarily a bad thing.

Some good advice is to have realistic goals, know your site conditions, and match these to your crops. It's okay to start small, whether you tuck some herbs into an ornamental bed or plant a fruit tree in a pot. A favorite combination of mine is a lime tree underplanted with mint—the makings of a mojito. Check to be sure that what you want to grow will thrive in your climate and with the available light.

I find that spending time in the garden is my preferred form of meditation, albeit a very active form. It is so completely engrossing that everything else falls away, and I never fail to feel happier and more content after spending time weeding, pruning, planting, or harvesting something I've grown.

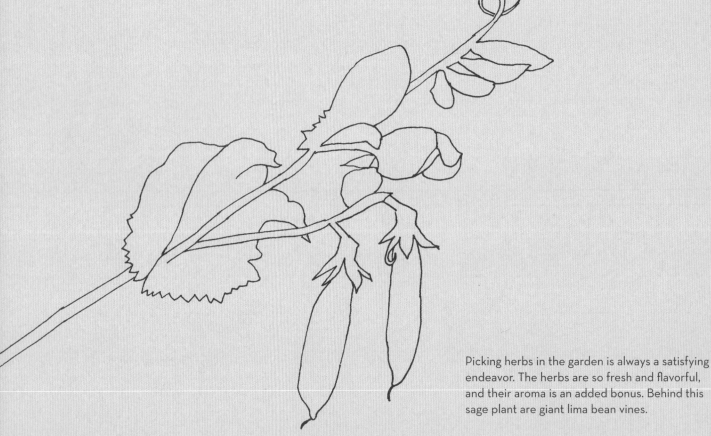

Picking herbs in the garden is always a satisfying endeavor. The herbs are so fresh and flavorful, and their aroma is an added bonus. Behind this sage plant are giant lima bean vines.

above: A simple concrete paver path set in a field of gravel serves as an informal entry to the garden. A raised bed creates a space for growing herbs and vegetables and a mixed cutting garden is planted against the house. Fragrant lavender and apricot-tinted roses, red and salmon Peruvian lily (*Alstroemeria*), and tall purple verbena (*Verbena bonariensis*) are underplanted with scented geraniums (*Pelargonium*).

left: I frequently incorporate edibles into ornamental beds. If you don't have the space or inclination to have a separate edible garden but want to snip some fresh herbs or pick a lemon, try this strategy.

opposite: Another strategy I often employ is to tuck raised beds behind ornamental planting or low hedges to visually mask the beds during less productive times.

above: Citrus trees respond beautifully to a one-inch layer of worm castings and regular fertilization. 'Oro Blanco' grapefruit yield a bright winter crop of intensely flavored fruit. I use the abundant harvest for marmalade, candied peel, and cocktails, or just pick one off the tree, cut it up, and eat it.

opposite: A good rule of thumb is to match plants with similar watering needs. However, a citrus tree that likes deep watering can live quite happily in the midst of plants with low water needs if put on drip irrigation or given an occasional drink from a slow hose.

EASY EATS FROM THE GARDEN

I have big culinary ambitions but little time. Here are some of my favorite quick, garden-inspired dishes.

ARUGULA SALAD Snip handfuls of arugula and toss with olive oil, fresh lemon juice, and sea salt. Add some roasted hazelnuts, a sliced persimmon or apple, and some blue cheese for a delicious salad.

FRUIT MIXER Juice grapefruit, or puree and strain berries, and add just a bit of simple syrup for sweetness. Serve over crushed ice with a splash of sparkling water or, better yet, a splash of gin. You can also put the juice-and-syrup combination in a baking pan and freeze it, scraping the surface every ten minutes to make a wonderful granita. Keep citrus rinds for making candied peel, which is a bit more labor-intensive but definitely worth the effort.

PRESERVED LEMONS Wash a bunch of lemons and cut four deep slits in each from top to bottom, without going all the way through. Fill the cuts with kosher salt and tightly pack a glass jar with the salted lemons. Sprinkle additional salt on top and store in a cool, dark place. After a couple of days, the lemons should be submerged in lemon juice; if not, add fresh lemon juice until the lemons are covered. In three to four weeks, they'll be ready to use—in stews, roast dishes, salads, and dressings.

SALSA VERDE Pick an assortment of herbs, including lots of leafy parsley. Chop with a clove of garlic and half a preserved lemon. Add olive oil, sea salt, and freshly ground pepper to make a stellar salsa verde, or, as my son calls it, "yummy green sauce."

CAPRESE SALAD Slice tomatoes and serve with burrata, good balsamic vinegar, olive oil, and lots of fresh basil. If you have an abundance of fresh tomatoes, slow roast them with thyme, olive oil, and sea salt until they're slightly caramelized; serve with crusty bread or over pasta.

GREEN SMOOTHIE Clip bunches of greens, like kale and spinach, and throw them into the blender with coconut water, dates or honey, mint, coconut butter, and a heaping spoonful of yogurt. Add crushed ice and blend for the freshest possible smoothie.

A kitchen garden leading to a ceramic studio is a study in edibles and ornamentals. Raised cedar beds are planted with a combination of greens, vegetables, and herbs, and a variety of fruit trees are planted throughout the garden. Native bay laurel provides screening and can be used for cooking.

top left: A bowl of freshly shelled beans, ready to be soaked and cooked. They can also be stored in an airtight container and will keep for months. I always save a few for replanting and to give to friends so they can grow their own.

top right: Freshly picked arugula has a spicy bite that pairs beautifully with other strong flavors. It is easy to grow from seeds or seedlings, and you can remove individual leaves to make a salad without needing to harvest the entire plant. A few plants can keep you in arugula for several weeks, or stagger your plantings to have greens for months.

right: In an artist's garden, twig towers provide necessary support for summer tomatoes, in addition to visual structure. Raised beds have the added benefit of lifting the work surface and making it easy to start off with good soil and drainage. Cedar is a great choice for raised beds as it is naturally resistant to rot, moisture, and insect damage.

For small spaces, balconies, and decks, pots planted
with herbs and greens are as pretty as they are useful.

above: Plastic buckets prefilled with water are a handy way of transporting freshly cut blooms. Shredded bark mulch makes neat paths throughout the garden.

right: Sherbet-colored ranunculus flowers resemble a ruffled petticoat.

opposite: High up in the hills at Silver Lake Farms, a growing field for flowers is a Technicolor dream. Set in the midst of rangy California oaks, olives, and newly planted fruit trees, staggered rows of vibrant flowers create a meandering stroll through what owner Tara Kolla describes as "organized, harmonious floriferous chaos."

above: Tara started with the sole idea of growing sweet peas and selling them at the farmers' market, but it wasn't until she grew her own that she discovered the bonus of their magnificent fragrance. She set up shop at our local farmers' market one spring, like a modern-day Eliza Doolittle, ready to sell her posies.

left: An old-fashioned bourbon rose has the most exquisite citrusy fragrance. Cut the stems when the buds just start to open up and in a day or two, the many layers of petals will unfold in a sumptuous display, perfuming whatever lucky space they inhabit.

opposite: It's always fun to grab a pair of clippers, head outside, and cut some flowers and foliage to make a homegrown arrangement. (Felco no. 6 is my favorite pruner.) I have a collection of vases in different sizes and colors, from bud vases for a little bedside-table nosegay to tall vessels for dramatic combinations of big leaves, branches, and leggy blooms.

top left: Beneficial insects, like ladybugs, are a great organic way of managing unwanted garden pests. Ladybugs come and stay of their own accord, if you create an appealing habitat for them by planting flowering perennials and annuals. They can also be purchased and released; just remember to wet down the area so they can have a welcoming drink and let them out in the early evening so they settle in for the night.

top right: Lure a dragonfly into your garden with a small water feature. Besides the obvious appeal of their ornamental quality, they do a bang-up job of banishing annoying bugs by snacking on mosquitoes, gnats, and midges.

left: Making compost is an easy task and is good for the environment. Instead of throwing out kitchen scraps and garden clippings, use one of several easy composting methods to make nutritious food for your garden.

opposite: Save seeds from your favorite edibles and flowers, like giant white lima beans, orange poppies, and Cavaillon melons, and share them with gardening friends.

opposite: What once was a dumping ground for broken-down cars and discarded mattresses has become a sanctuary for more than twenty-five beehives and their buzzing inhabitants. My friend Max shares her garden with her husband, Steve, a couple of cats, a school of koi, a two-legged turtle, and a hundred-thousand wild bees. Their numbers may sound vast, but after spending a sunny summer day in her garden, you'll find that her bees are the most polite roommates you could possibly imagine.

top: Like people, bees and their hives have different personalities. This bunch is affectionately characterized by their beekeeper as "really artistic and messy."

bottom: Max humbly describes herself as "not the best beekeeper, but good enough." Last spring's harvest yielded one hundred pounds of delicious amber honey, which was decanted into specimen jars and labeled Sticky Acres.

above: Different breeds of chickens, such as Aracaunas, Rhode Island Reds, and Silkies, lay eggs of different colors and sizes. Pasture-raised eggs are better for your health, as they are lower in cholesterol and fat and higher in vitamins and omega-3 fatty acids—plus, they taste delicious.

opposite: Chickens make a great addition to an active garden. Besides providing fresh eggs, they are natural experts at making fertilizer that can be used throughout the garden. Their diet consists of table scraps, garden clippings, and any bugs they find, and they are surprisingly sociable when they've been raised around people.

Purple Sage
Salvia officinalis 'Purpurea'

Barbeque Rosemary
Rosmarinus officinalis 'Barbeque'

Purple Basil
Ocimum basilicum 'Purpurascens'

East Indian Lemongrass
Cymbopogon flexuosus

Artichoke
Cynara scolymus

Golden Oregano
Origanum vulgare 'Aureum'

Edibles to Incorporate into the Garden

Chives
Allium schoenoprasum

Bay Laurel
Laurus nobilis

Nagami Kumquat
Fortunella margarita 'Nagami'

Bronze Fennel
Foeniculum vulgare 'Purpureum'

Magenta Spreen Lambsquarter
Chenopodium giganteum

Black Jack Fig
Ficus carica 'Black Jack'

An easy way to get started growing edibles is to integrate them into ornamental planting areas.
Here are some of my favorite edible plants that are beautiful to look at and easy to grow.

Purple Coneflower
Echinacea purpurea 'Magnus'

Ring of Fire Sunflower
Helianthus annuus 'Ring of Fire'

Santa Barbara Sage
Salvia leucantha 'Santa Barbara'

Mediterranean Spurge
Euphorbia characias wulfenii

Pincushion Flower
Scabiosa caucasica

Yarrow
Achillea millefolium 'Cassis'

Easy Flowers for Cutting

Red Kangaroo Paw
Anigozanthos 'Red Cross'

Green Goddess Calla Lily
Zantedeschia 'Green Goddess'

Cornflower
Centaurea cyanus

Peruvian Lily
Alstroemeria 'The Third Harmonic'

Breadseed Poppy
Papaver 'Raspberry Breadseed'

Bird of Paradise
Strelitzia reginae

Cutting flowers from my own garden is a simple pleasure. Many flowers don't require special care to produce lots of blooms over a long season and can be grown as part of an ornamental planting or even in a pot.

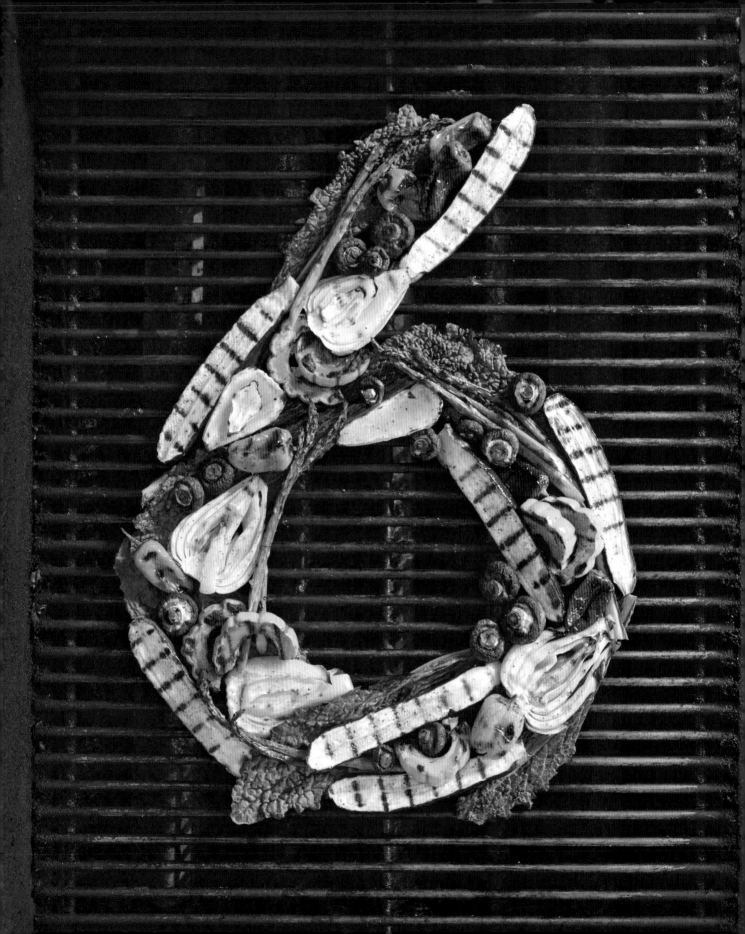

COOKING
IN THE GARDEN

I made a discovery one memorable evening—cooking and garden design are profoundly linked for me. I was trying to figure out how to supplement my income as a painter and had a novel idea. Since I loved to cook, I decided to open a restaurant one night a week for the summer. The setting for this grand experiment was my own back garden.

The menu was prix fixe: a three-course meal along the lines of a backyard Chez Panisse, but with a simple home-cooked meal that was mostly grilled outside. My friends pitched in and helped hang lights, loaned silverware, and hauled in huge bags of organic produce that I had purchased at the farmers' market. A chef friend ordered free-range chickens for me and kept the carcasses for stock. On opening night, with a pounding heart and running on pure adrenaline, I unlocked my gate and people started to pour in. Soon the wine was flowing, the conversation reached the perfect low roar, and hors d'oeuvres were passed around the pool.

At around 9:30 P.M. a friend nudged me and whispered, "Are you going to serve dinner soon?" In my excitement I had completely lost track of the time. I asked my three dozen guests to take their seats at the tables scattered throughout the garden and rounded up my tiny waitstaff to begin service. "How should the plate look?" one asked. I was completely floored for a moment. Having never worked in a restaurant, the extent of my behind-the-scenes experience was nil. I had eaten at restaurants, hundreds, if not thousands, of times, so I had assumed that I would naturally intuit what was involved. I was wrong.

I improvised the arrangement: "Black beans at three o'clock! Grilled vegetables at six, mesclun salad at nine, grilled chicken at midnight! Cilantro sauce on top of the chicken. Now go!" Out the plates went.

Among my guests that evening was a friend with a new house. By the time dinner was served, he had commissioned me to create a garden. He liked what he saw in mine: a lush palette of ornamental grasses, gold lantana and fuchsia bougainvillea, fragrant Japanese honeysuckle, and citrus trees heavy with fruit, all wrapped around a series of simple terraced patios. He wanted me to start on his garden the next day, but I told him it needed to be the day after, as I had dishes to wash. My restaurant lasted exactly one more week, the grand closing as rollicking as the grand opening, and very suddenly, and most unexpectedly, I was in the landscape business.

Not a summer goes by without someone asking if I'll start up my backyard restaurant again, and, while I still love to cook using the freshest possible ingredients, I think my restaurant days are long behind me. We grill year-round, and there are few meals that don't include some clipped herbs or fresh lemon from our bountiful tree. There is an alchemy to cooking that is compelling. You take a bunch of raw ingredients, chop, season, mix them up, maybe apply some heat—and if all goes well, you have something delicious to eat. Sitting down to a home-cooked meal is one of the most satisfying and important moments in a day, and, for many people it is something that would be hard to live without.

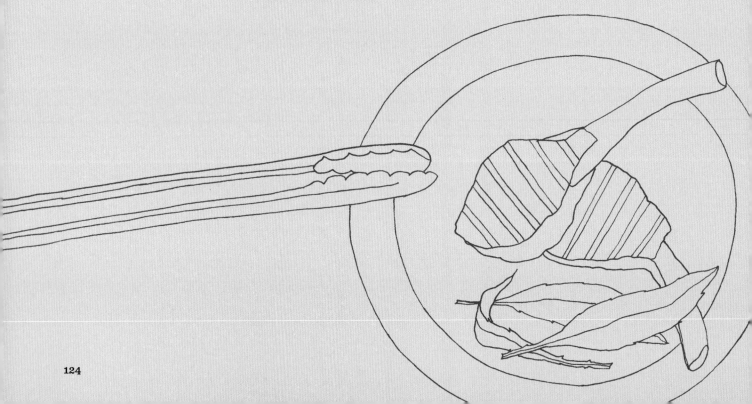

top left: Wrapping fish with fig leaves is a wonderful method of retaining moisture and infusing the fish with the subtle fragrance of the fig tree.

top right: I like to tuck in some other aromatics to enhance the flavor, like French thyme (*Thymus vulgaris*) and pink peppercorns from our California pepper tree (*Schinus molle*).

right: It's easy to use fig leaves as wrappers. Wash them gently, pat them dry, and rub them with a bit of olive oil. Fold the leaves over the fish and knit the ends together with a toothpick, and you're ready to grill.

top left: One of my favorite gifts to give is a fruit picker. The telescoping pole with a little cage on the end helps you reach fruit high up in the tree and easily pluck it off.

top right: If you have a lemon tree, preserved lemons (see page 104) are super easy to make and will add bright citrus flavor to dishes year-round.

left: Giant white beans grown at home were left to dry in their shells, then harvested and cooked until tender. Tossed with crispy bacon, garlic, chili flakes, and lots of fresh fried sage, they make a great accompaniment to grilled meats and garden greens.

opposite: The stylish outdoor kitchen at William T. Georgis's home includes a smoker and a floating countertop for nearby dining. Lighting for the kitchen counter was smartly integrated into the wood backsplash.

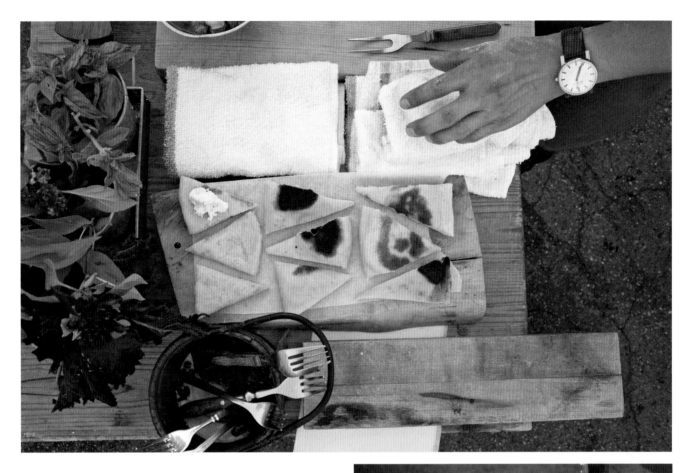

above: An asphalt parking lot has been transformed into a verdant culinary mecca by chefs Tara Maxey and Matt Poley of Heirloom LA. Herbs from their garden are kept in small pots of water to keep them fresh. Take a tip from the pros: Set up all your ingredients and a work surface right next to your grill.

right: Cast-iron pans are a brilliant way to cook over very high heat on a charcoal grill.

opposite: Mark Stambler, a passionate bread baker, likes to make rustic French-style loaves in his homemade wood-burning oven. A straw basket is used to cool and transport his freshly baked bread to appreciative family and friends, and the smell is as divine as the taste.

APPLYING HEAT

Figuring out your needs for outdoor cooking is the first step. For the ultimate experience, install a built-in grill or oven with a generous countertop for prep and serving. Check your local laws regarding outdoor cooking. Some areas have regulations regarding the proximity of heat sources to structures, as well as restrictions on burning wood.

GAS GRILLS These trump other cooking options when it comes to convenience. You can light the grill and start cooking in less than ten minutes. Freestanding grills come with refillable tanks or, if you have a permanent location for your grill, you can have a professional run a gas line to that spot, making tanks unnecessary.

CHARCOAL GRILLS Cooking over charcoal imparts food with great smoky flavor. The classic Weber grill can't be beat when it comes to no-frills outdoor cooking, and a charcoal starter speeds up the process of getting coals hot. Mini grills are fun for tabletop use and perfect for small spaces.

CERAMIC GRILLS/SMOKERS These offer a vast range of cooking possibilities, from low-and-slow temperatures for smoking to very high heat for pizza. They are coveted by serious cooks.

ROTISSERIES If you like to be hands-off while grilling, a rotisserie attachment is the ideal accessory. Just skewer your meat onto a spit and the rotation will evenly roast large cuts and whole birds. Add a pan underneath to catch the drippings for a sauce or throw in some root vegetables for a delicious side dish.

WOOD-BURNING OVENS These are for people interested in the most primordial and skilled form of cooking. You can make your own or purchase one of the many professional-grade ovens available. Use these to bake bread and pizza, as well as to roast meats, vegetables, and fruits (a new favorite of mine is roasted dates with olive oil and sea salt).

SOLAR OVENS The greenest option, these use the sun as the heat source. While not for those in a rush or looking for some char, the process is similar to using a Crock-Pot and the results are just as succulent. Great for stews, soups, fish, vegetables, breads, and cakes.

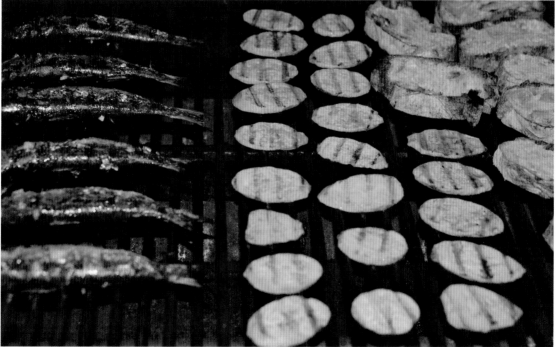

top: A cast-iron hibachi grill is perfect for small spaces and a fun way to cook out in the garden.

bottom: Gas grills are wonderful for quick and easy results and minimal cleanup. Whole meals can be cooked in one go, like this dinner of fresh sardines, summer squash, and crusty bread.

top left: This dramatic technique for cooking mussels, known as *éclade de moules*, is a specialty of the Charentais region of France but can be duplicated anywhere. All you need is a flat piece of wood, some fig leaves, a mound of dried pine needles, and a bunch of mussels. The mussels are laid in concentric circles, hinge side up, over a solid layer of the leaves.

top right: A thick layer of pine needles are mounded over the mussels and lit in multiple places. Wet down the surrounding area first, if you live in a dry zone. After a couple of minutes, the fire will die out and the mussels will be cooked. Pick them up carefully and eat immediately with crusty bread, butter, and a glass of white wine. Prepare to swoon.

left: Grilling bread and dates over a fire pit is an adventurous and delicious way to start a meal.

opposite: Cornish game hens are beautifully roasted on a spit over a pan of beets and herbs. This method doesn't require lots of tending to the grill. I always check the internal temperature with a meat thermometer to ensure the birds are properly cooked.

Chef Kristin Ferguson built her pizza oven by hand, following instructions from a paperback called *Build Your Own Earth Oven*. Set at the back of the garden, amid free-roaming chickens and fruit trees, the oven is made of cob, which is a combination of sand, clay, and straw. Temperatures can reach a searing 1,200°F and pizzas cook in less than three minutes. The results are more than impressive and completely delicious.

Cooking Outdoors in a Wood-burning Oven

Kristin crafts garden-inspired pizzas, like her Allium pie, topped with a variety of roots from the onion family, and the pizza pictured above—an exquisite combination of oven-roasted cauliflower, brandy-soaked raisins, hazelnuts, cream, Gruyère, and garlic confit. Fire master/husband Harmon recommends using hard woods, like almond and fruit woods, for high temperatures. Make sure to watch out for your eyes and eyebrows—Kristin wears protective goggles to protect hers from heat and smoke.

Cooking with wood fire imparts food with the most incredible flavor. Making pizza is a fun group event—prepare lots of different toppings and let people assemble their own pies.

ART IN THE LANDSCAPE

The union of gardens and art has not been an easy one for me. When I started designing gardens, the idea was that it would be my day job. For that reason alone, I wanted to keep a distance between what I did outside for others and what I did in the studio. I thought making gardens was design and painting was art, and that the two should be kept separate, like church and state.

Over the years I've changed my tune. The lines between design and art blurred long ago. Never before has there been such a pervasive and inclusive mash-up of art, design, music, film, and fashion. Why not include landscape design in the cultural cocktail, extra dry with a twist?

I've had the great fortune to make gardens for many highly creative people, including designers, artists, writers, filmmakers, photographers, and musicians. These projects have a special kind of chemistry that I particularly enjoy. Sometimes it's about creating a dynamic new context for a piece of art, breaking away from the neutral white box. Other times there's a shared vision of creating an outdoor environment that is unique or completely unexpected, like a hillside tapestry or a black-and-silver lunar-inspired landscape. Complex plant combinations with distinct color palettes are one of my primary forms of creative expression. I've found that many of my favorite gardens are by artists who treat their entire outdoor spaces as sites for experimentation. Since gardens are by their very nature a fabrication—a human manipulation of the natural world—they afford great opportunities for artistic license.

Most landscape painting finds inspiration from the natural landscape, understandably, but I have found great inspiration for my paintings from artworks focusing on the constructed landscape, like Claude Monet's magnificent garden at Giverny. A visit there is akin to stepping into one of his lovely paintings. Amedeo Modigliani's potent portraits of hothouse flowers served as a basis for the color palettes in a series of my own paintings, and Karl Blossfeldt's rigorous photographic studies of plants and flowers influenced the forms and shapes in my work. Representations of the natural world inspired my work on canvas, and now my canvas is the natural world.

My gardens share the same elements as my paintings and explore color, form, and scale, along with the addition of texture, seasonality, and the exciting wild card of nature at play. Most interesting, one of the greatest differences is that gardens are not flat surfaces, but three-dimensional ones. As much as I love paintings, you can only enter them in your mind, whereas a garden is a real space that you can truly inhabit. I love to wrap patio spaces and walkways with lush and exuberant plantings. I relish the experience of being pressed up against the plants, so you can enjoy their detail, nuance, and fragrance. I find that to evoke this level of engagement in a garden is one of the most compelling aspects of the art of landscape design.

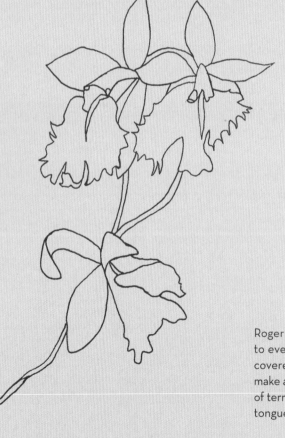

Roger Herman and Eika Aoshima bring their artistry to everything they do, and the arrangement of their covered terrace is no exception. Roger's bold ceramics make a perfect counterpoint to Eika's linear arrangement of terra-cotta pots planted with graphic mother-in-law's tongue (*Sanseviera trifasciata*).

this page: The painter Roger Herman is also known for his spectacular ceramics, and his garden looks as if it has sprung from the same sensibility. There is a sense of discovery and delight when you stumble across one of his pieces outside, and their striking forms perfectly complement the rugged plants. Each pot has its own distinct personality; some are quite provocative while others are playful.

opposite: The wild beauty of this garden makes it one of my favorite places to visit. When not being used for meals and parties, a generous tiled table displays a selection of pots. The mixed planting along the fence line creates a soft delineation between private and public spaces, so that the boundary between the garden and the adjacent park is blurred.

left: The delicate steel casting of an apple tree and fallen fruit by sculptor Rona Pondick is set amid a vibrant planting of chartreuse-flowering Mediterranean spurge (*Euphorbia characias wulfenii*) and Goodwin Creek gray lavender (*Lavandula dentata* 'Goodwin Creek Gray'). The garden around the sculpture was designed primarily using plants mentioned in the Bible, with the occasional creative interpretation.

right: A giant slab of granite provides a quiet perch to contemplate the garden and its sculptures, while resembling a sculpture itself. An entire street lane had to be closed on the busiest part of Wilshire Boulevard to stage the crane that lifted the heavy stone into place.

opposite: Period marks the spot. An avid art collector punctuates his garden with a giant period by the artist Fiona Banner. Installed on a raised platform of decomposed granite, the shiny black orb reflects the surrounding garden, including the strappy foliage of bronze flax (*Phormium tenax* 'Atropurpureum').

ELEMENTS OF DESIGN

When creating gardens I give a great deal of attention to composition. Here are several important elements to consider when designing. If you want great results, the key is making choices with intention.

COLOR Create a color-focused palette, pulling images from books, magazines, or the Internet, when selecting flowers, foliage, stone, tile, and fabrics, and look at them together to see how well they work. An inspiration board, either real or virtual, is a priceless tool in the design process.

TEXTURE Combine a variety of textures to highlight the quality of each element. Think about putting hard with soft, feathery with static, and shiny with matte.

FORM I like to pair the organic forms of plants with rectilinear walls, patios, and walkways. Combine sculptural plant forms with leafy mounds for interest and contrast.

SCALE Play with a range of sizes and don't be afraid to use a big element in a small space. It will add drama and make the space feel bigger, like using one huge gorgeous pot with a large plant rather than lots of little ones.

SEASONALITY Embrace the seasons and include foliage that changes color. Stagger bloom cycles of flowers and grasses for year-round interest. Enjoy seed heads and dramatic branching in cool months, and the onset of new buds and leaves in warm months.

SOUND AND MOVEMENT Gardens are dynamic environments. The crunch of gravel, the splash of water, the rustle of bamboo, and the chirping of birds all enhance the experience.

A combination of cool and warm tones with tall static forms and smaller grass-like blades paints a vivid picture.

above: In the midst of a dramatic canyon setting, the artists Lari Pittman and Roy Dowell have created exacting gridded compositions of their favorite plants, much like the meticulous order and beauty of their individual paintings and prints.

right: The vertical structure of Peruvian apple cactus (*Cereus peruvianus*) beautifully offsets the prickly orbs of golden barrel cactus (*Echinocactus grusonii*).

top left: The designer Sabrina Judge uses color to great effect. Icy blue century plant (*Agave americana*) is beautifully paired with other true-blue friends, like blue chalksticks (*Senecio serpens*) and blue fescue (*Festuca glauca*). The feathery texture of the grass is a wonderful counterpoint to the sculptural forms of the succulents in this tone-on-tone planting, a striking composition against the crimson wall.

top right: A bare wall can be like a blank canvas in a garden. The combination of purple wandering Jew (*Tradescantia pallida* 'Purple Heart') and metallic echeveria (*Echeveria gibbiflora* 'Metallica') pops brilliantly against the tangerine wall.

left: An inhabitable sculpture by the artist Adam Mason is thoughtfully sited to take in the view. The rectilinear geometry and bold color stand in stark relief to the rustic setting of Laura Cooper and Nick Taggart's garden.

opposite: A green roof planted with succulents works like a flat canvas. My love of abstract pour paintings from the 1960s inspired the swirling patterns and graphic treatment.

The branching of the Hong Kong orchid tree (*Bauhinia blakeana*) naturally frames artist Dora De Larios's ceramic figurine, creating a beautiful composition in this enchanting landscape by Sabrina Judge.

The garden courtyard at Isabel Marant's shop is a chromatic study in shades of green. Color tones transition from the light center to the dark edges, simulating dappled sunlight, all set in brilliant relief against the charcoal pebble ground cover.

left: The living works of artist Robert Cannon offer a new perspective on sculpture set in a natural outdoor environment. Collectively named Terraforms, the sculptures are intended to grow and change with the seasons.

right: Constructed of hollow concrete shells and packed with earth to create small planting pockets, this Terraform provokes the question of what happens when the sculpture is cared for, or neglected, as a stand-in for the greater environment.

left: A magnificent ceramic piece by artist Michael Arntz holds prize placement in a front courtyard. An edited palette of blue-gray succulents and finely textured dark green perennials complement the earthy finish and clean form of the sculpture. My impulse is to plant big things in small spaces.

right: A kinetic bronze sculpture from the 1950s that moves with water is a delightful centerpiece in a sculptural garden.

above: The organic work of California sculptor Stan Bitters creates an experience of wonder and whimsy in the garden. His monumental ceramic medallions resemble magnificent flowers and appear to be sprouting out of the ground.

right: Bitters's earthy terra-cotta birdhouses captivate humans as well as feathered creatures.

Majestic clusters of Bitters's totems make horticultural friends with an equally impressive stand of timber bamboo, adjacent to a teahouse in a landscape designed by Jose Rodriguez.

above: Artist Pae White celebrates nature by making a series of cast-iron sculptures in the playful shapes of local fauna.

left: The surprise of the sculptures is that fully functional grills are tucked inside.

opposite: A striking pair of bird cage sculptures greets visitors at the entrance to Pae's home. People are not the only species who appreciate the work; Pae frequently finds that small birds build their nests within the wire forms to protect their offspring from hawks and crows.

Powis Castle Artemisia
Artemisia 'Powis Castle'

Sweet Potato Vine
Ipomoea batatas 'Blackie'

Golden Prayers Hosta
Hosta 'Golden Prayers'

Crème Brûlée Coral Bells
Heuchera 'Crème Brûlée'

All Gold Japanese Forest Grass
Hakonechloa macra 'All Gold'

Copper Spoons
Kalanchoe orgyalis

Plants with Metallic Foliage

New Zealand Hair Sedge
Carex tenuiculmis 'Cappuccino'

Licorice Plant
Helichrysum petiolare

Gryphon Begonia
Begonia 'Gryphon'

Pink Iceplant
Oscularia deltoides

Golden Breath of Heaven
Coleonema pulchellum 'Sunset Gold'

Cranesbill
Geranium 'Dusky Crug'

There is much more to the world of plants than just shades of green. Foliage comes in a rainbow of colors, but to add real depth to a planting, try some metallic tones of bronze, silver, or gold.

PLACES FOR PLAY

Easter began early with our son, Ian, delighting over having found a chocolate bunny wrapped with a bow at his bedside. He crawled into our bed for a drowsy cuddle and I crept downstairs to begin our preparations for the day. The lunch menu was vividly green, a happy accident celebrating the onset of spring: roasted asparagus, parsley salad, a verdant spinach frittata, and freshly made guacamole from avocados shared by a neighbor with a bountiful tree.

It was a hot day, unusually so for Easter Sunday. Everyone brought swimsuits and the kids were soon in the pool, despite its frigid temperature of 60°F. Ian ran around, jumping in with floppy cannonballs, and his friend Max's lower lip turned a light shade of violet from the cold. Soon they were laid out on towels on top of the warm stone deck, sunning themselves for a moment before the day's main event. The kids decorated a couple dozen eggs and my husband, Erik, and I hid them around the garden. We had two rules: no pushing or shoving, and, as the eggs were hidden in plain sight, no trampling on any plants to find them. The hunt was on. Every hard-boiled egg found could be traded in for a small foil-wrapped chocolate one—the old-fashioned kind that I remembered from my childhood. After lunch, the kids ran around and played happily in the garden and the grown-ups hung out at the kitchen table and talked, enjoying the remainder of the day.

Children need play, plain and simple run-around-the-yard spontaneous play. They need unstructured time to explore, imagine, and create. Lack of play is one epidemic in this country that can be easily remedied. It doesn't require any miraculous drugs, new legislation, or abundance of funding, and the importance of play cannot be underestimated. It is essential for helping children develop, flourish, and succeed—and most adults could use a dose as well.

Space, of course, can be a determining factor in what you can do. A frequent client request is to make driveways and parking areas double as play spaces, so that they can be used for basketball, bike riding, scootering, and skating. A box of chalk for drawing on hardscape or making a hopscotch court can provide hours of fun. One driveway I made out of decomposed granite doubles as a boules court, a game that can be enjoyed by the whole family. Open lawn areas are perfect for croquet, badminton, and volleyball, or timeless games like Duck, Duck, Goose, Hide and Seek, and Simon Says. On a nice day, bring out a deck of cards and a backgammon or chess set, and enjoy open-air play, as dozens of Parisians do in Luxembourg Gardens each day.

I encounter more and more people who share a fresh approach and mind-set toward outdoor recreation and take an active role in making engaging spaces to share with their kids. It is wonderful to participate in creating an environment or an activity that cultivates imagination and nurtures confidence, and I see how much it adds to people's lives, at any age. But I think our son summed it up best when I asked him what he thought was important about play. He said, "It's not so much that it's important, it's fun!"

A small patch of sod is great to have for little ones but playing in the yard isn't just running around the lawn anymore. Kids (and grown-ups!) love to play outside in all kinds of creative ways, from eccentric playhouses to a variety of delightful outdoor games.

above: A romantic playhouse, lovingly made by artists Nick Taggart and Laura Cooper for their daughter, is sited in the midst of their magical garden. Giving a child a place of his or her own encourages imagination and helps to build confidence.

right: I like to have the kids decorate the eggs and the adults hide them as part of the fun of an Easter egg hunt.

opposite: A canvas teepee tucked into the base of a cluster of sycamore trees makes the perfect getaway for young and old alike. Simple precast round pavers lead the way through verdant planting, and the canopy of the trees keeps the tent cool.

left: The Gingerbread Pirate Ship is the madcap creation of Bradley Thordarson, and the centerpiece of what he calls a "learning landscape" that he and his wife, Michelle, made for their children. Nothing is precious—everything in the garden is intended to grow, shift, and evolve with the needs of their family.

right: Crafting a narrative can be a meaningful part of the experience. The spiky yucca that looms over the fort is a prickly sea monster rising to attack the ship. The hillside, on which the ship is perched, is the crest of a wave, and the ship is heading toward home. Ahoy, matey!

opposite: An idea sparked first by an architectural model evolved to become Knit Fort. A series of modular wood elements that fit together with rubber cord creates a flexible and semi-transparent structure. Matt Gagnon built the fort as a prototype and tests it out frequently by enjoying it with his wife and two sons.

opposite and left: An old-fashioned tire swing never gets boring. Strung from an apple tree in a meadow, this swing could not be more simple or compelling.

right: Nestled amid ornamental grasses, a warm-weather igloo makes for a sophisticated yet kid-friendly playhouse. This imaginative work from the landscape architectural firm Surfacedesign, Inc., was inspired by the desire for a structure that wouldn't be quickly outgrown.

GREAT PLAY SURFACES

There are a myriad of surfaces that can be used in a garden for different kinds of recreation. Here are some options to explore.

LAWNS In climates that don't require irrigation water, old-fashioned lawns are hard to beat as a friendly all-around play surface. Practice organic maintenance and invest in good ground prep to improve your surface and drainage.

SYNTHETIC LAWNS In arid climates, synthetic lawns provide a great surface for play without requiring water, maintenance, or chemicals—plus, they never go dormant in the winter. Keep in mind that they can get hot in full summer sun.

MEADOWS These grasses provide a thick green carpet with low water and maintenance needs. Plugs can take time to grow in but there are now some varieties that can be laid down like sod.

DECOMPOSED GRANITE Fine-crushed stone makes the perfect surface for games like boules and horseshoes, and will be a smooth enough surface for riding bikes and scooters.

PLAY MATS Rubber matting works beautifully under play sets and swings for a soft, forgiving surface. It's available in tiles or can be installed as one piece.

HARD SURFACES Concrete is the best surface for basketball and games like four square, and is ideal for anything with wheels. Bring out colored chalk and you have a great drawing surface as well. Stone is also good, if you prefer a more natural material.

A trampoline is ingeniously set into a series of rolling mounds, creating a dynamic and beautiful play area. While flat lawns are good for playing more structured games, a little topography can provide its own amusement. This garden was designed by Surfacedesign, Inc. One of the firm's principals, James Lord, explains, "So much is handed to kids, but this makes them use their imagination."

above: Croquet, a timeless sport in which a wooden ball is hit through hoops, or "wickets," with a mallet, has been enjoyed for generations. Besides being a great way to develop hand-eye coordination, it's addictively fun.

left: For those who prefer to watch people at play, comfortable seating courtside is always welcome.

opposite: The game of pétanque, also known as boules, is best played on a surface of decomposed granite under the shade of a tree. The object is to throw hollow metal balls as close as possible to a small wooden ball called a *cochonnet*, which means "piglet." It can also be played on packed earth, gravel, grass, or sand.

top left: A rolling meadow was planted in lieu of lawn as a low-water and low-maintenance organic play surface. A combination of hard and soft paths form an informal loop around the property, linking the different spaces together for dynamic circulation.

top right: A little water can provide a lot of pleasure. A large glazed pot made into a water feature is a focal element in the garden. Water is always a fun element in which to play.

left: A pull ring turns on the faucet so that buckets and watering cans can be easily filled by little and big hands alike.

opposite: For the enjoyment of a young family, we designed a generous play area nestled into a steep hillside. A retractable awning creates shade on demand, and plenty of built-in seating ensures everyone has a comfortable place to perch.

THE JOY OF RELAXATION

It was a hot and gorgeous Saturday, so my son, Ian, and I decided to make some lemonade. We went out to our lemon tree and picked a dozen. While he juiced the fruit, I made simple syrup by boiling some sugar with water for a few minutes. I cooled off the syrup in the freezer, and then combined it with the lemon juice and some water.

This is something we do quite often, but what happened next was a new twist. Ian took a glass, put in some crushed ice and a couple sprigs of fresh mint, and filled the glass with lemonade. He took his glass outside. I heard the sound of the umbrella crank turning, then it was quiet. A few minutes went by. I went outside and found Ian enjoying his drink poolside, lounging in a chaise under the canopy of the striped canvas umbrella. He invited me to join him on the adjacent chaise and suggested that I too get a glass because it would be "refreshing." I almost fell over.

Ian, who was about to turn six at the time, understands the meaning of relaxation. He gets that it's enjoyable to sit outside with a cool drink and spend time by himself or with another person. It's that simple. I, on the other hand, see every day as a race against time, and have to remind myself to slow down occasionally and enjoy a quiet moment. So I joined him. I felt the warm sun on my legs, smelled the grapefruit blossoms, watched the rippling motion of the blue water, and had a delightful conversation with my boy.

Relaxation, which by many has been perceived as an indulgence, is now considered an essential component to a well-balanced and productive life. A significant part of my job is creating beautiful environments that inspire others to relax. One project that highlighted this wish was the grounds for a new boutique hotel in Palm Springs called the Parker. People go to the Parker to take a break, unwind, and enjoy themselves, and it was my job to design the outdoor spaces, a total of ten acres, to create and maximize guests' opportunity to do just that.

The conceit for the Parker was brilliant. Design maven Jonathan Adler and I were asked to remake the hotel into something that would be imagined as the private estate of an eccentric Auntie Mame–type character named Mrs. Parker. We were instructed to create a destination that we would want to go to ourselves, so we let the fun begin. My focus was on the makeover of the grounds—in place of the anemic roses, drooping snapdragons, and half-dead boxwood hedges that had been spray-painted green throughout the property, I envisioned a lush transformation that had yet to be experienced in this desert climate. I designed a series of linked garden rooms, each with its own identity and opportunity to kick back. Macramé hammocks were strung up from the trunks of handsome date palms, and cozy seating nooks were tucked into the plantings. Moroccan lanterns hung from languid pepper trees and the sound of burbling water provided a soothing soundtrack. Jonathan designed a fun and chic pool cabana for the new pool area and I had a pair of chin-high antique Foo dogs shipped from China to go poolside. Various types of engaging recreation were incorporated into the grounds, including areas to play boules, croquet, and tennis. Lavender, citrus blossoms, and California sage perfumed the air. Over the years, countless people have come to me seeking to create the same experience they had at the Parker. I couldn't agree with them more. Sometimes the most relaxing thing you can do is to stay right at home.

above: A generous steel fire pit in the desert can warm a crowd on cool winter evenings. Classic butterfly chairs remain a favorite choice, as they're easy to move around, the covers can be washed, and they can be stacked and stored if needed.

left: Cotton hammocks strung up between date palms (*Phoenix dactylifera*) offer an island-feel getaway in the midst of the desert. It's ideal to site your hammock over a soft surface like lawn, especially if it will be used by children.

above: At our home, a pair of upholstered chairs always invites relaxation. Tough outdoor fabrics, like Sunbrella, ensure that your cushions will be long lived and easy to clean.

right: Privacy is key to making a place feel relaxing, particularly around a pool. A large stand of Mexican weeping bamboo (*Otatea acuminata*) is nestled beween two carrotwood trees (*Cupaniopsis anacardioides*) to provide dense screening and visual interest in a narrow space along our property line.

left: Chaises don't necessarily need to be poolside. A vintage chaise on a raised wood deck, tucked under the canopy of a gold medallion tree (*Cassia leptophylla*), is a lovely place to relax off a master bedroom.

right: Ornamental grasses move gently with a little air current. Use easy-to-care-for plants, like succulents, so your garden is a respite from chores, rather than a chore itself.

opposite: A giant daybed is a favorite destination to curl up with the newspaper, chat with a friend, or better yet, take a nap.

above: A gracious seating area facing a beautiful view is a great spot for relaxing at the end of the day. Plant a variety of French lavender to infuse your garden with calming fragrance.

left: A layered planting provides lots of interest and minimal maintenance, needing only a winter cutback once a year. Agave 'Blue Glow', prostrate wooly grevillea (*Grevillea lanigera* 'Prostrate Form'), oriental fountain grass (*Pennisetum orientale*), and blue sage (*Salvia clevelandii* 'Winnifred Gilman') frame the view. The California native sage releases a divine herbal scent when warmed by the sun.

above: Gas fire pits are user-friendly—just turn them on and kick back. I always like to include large lava rocks to capture the heat and radiate warmth.

right: Hummingbirds never tire of orange kangaroo paws (*Anigozanthos* 'Orange Cross') and I couldn't agree more—just sit back and watch the show. These willowy stalks make great cutting flowers for enjoying inside as well.

CREATE A CALMING ENVIRONMENT

Take a few steps to inspire use and enjoyment of your outdoor spaces, without having to run around every time you want to relax outside. Here are a few that I recommend.

COMFORTABLE SEATING This is key. Include a cozy chair or a cushy chaise in your setup, or, if you have the room, a big daybed on which you can read a book or take a nap.

ANTICIPATE YOUR NEEDS If you like shade, keep an umbrella set up for sunny days. If you tend to get cold, include a heater or fire pit in the mix.

KEEP TOWELS ON HAND If you have a pool or spa, be sure to have a stack of towels at the ready.

INCLUDE A WATER FEATURE Tuck a concrete bowl or glazed pot outfitted with a small fountain pump into a discreet spot to provide a naturally relaxing soundtrack. The sound of water is very soothing.

INSTALL SPEAKERS Make it easy to listen to music by placing unobtrusive weather-resistant speakers outside.

CREATE RELAXING RITUALS Make a habit of having a cup of tea in the morning in your garden as part of starting your day, or enjoying a glass of wine outside when you get home from work. Have a dip in your spa or relax for a moment by your fire pit before bedtime.

PRIVACY AND SHELTER String up a shade sail, put out an umbrella, or plant a tree to create a canopy to screen out neighbors and create a personal Shangri-la.

left: Taking an outdoor shower is an exhilarating way to start your day. In collaboration with Montalba Architects, we created this sleek open air design that allows you to experience the sky and trees in the midst of dense planting yet provides ample privacy.

right: Bathing alfresco in an old claw-foot tub is a delightful way to unwind in the garden of Laura Cooper and Nick Taggart. Use biodegradable soap and attach a hose, for an easy gray water system that will water the garden when you're done with your bath.

left: A discreet path leads to an intimate getaway at the bottom of a hillside property. Perfect for when you're in a Greta Garbo mood and want to be alone.

right: A giant daybed with bolsters is a great place to unwind by yourself or with a partner. Small ceramic ottomans on which to set books, glasses, or a drink can be moved around the garden on an as-needed basis.

opposite: A patio at the end of the pool is an intimate spot for relaxing poolside. The double-wide chaise fits snugly in the compact space and a trio of lanterns hang from the branches of the tree. A couple of pots and ceramic ottomans complete the scene.

left: The smooth lawn extends the sense of space beyond the patio, and low planting frames the view toward the ocean and sunset.

above: Blue chalksticks (*Senecio serpens*), yellow-striped dwarf variegated flax (*Phormium* 'Duet'), and orange-flowering kangaroo paws (*Anigozanthos* 'Orange Cross') create a subtle variety of colors, forms, and textures, all within a small scale.

above: My friends and collaborators—architect/interior designer William T. Georgis and art curator Richard Marshall—embrace outdoor living with high style in their chic La Jolla garden. A pergola above an outdoor dining area also houses heaters, perfect for cool coastal evenings, and a hanging light illuminates the scene.

right: Low-growing succulents soften the thick-cut travertine stair treads in this cozy nook, carved into the hillside. Georgis's outdoor furnishings for the garden have the same exacting attention to detail as his exquisite interiors.

Star Jasmine
Trachelospermum jasminoides

Blue Sage
Salvia clevelandii 'Winnifred Gilman'

Cecile Brunner Climbing Rose
Rosa 'Cecile Brunner'

Black Knight Butterfly Bush
Buddleja davidii 'Black Knight'

Hall's Japanese Honeysuckle
Lonicera japonica 'Halliana'

Black Knight Sweet Pea
Lathyrus odoratus 'Black Knight'

Fragrant Plants

Chocolate Vine
Akebia quinata

Angel's Trumpet
Brugmansia 'Charles Grimaldi'

Rose Geranium
Pelargonium graveolens

Tangerine Beauty Crossvine
Bignonia capreolata 'Tangerine Beauty'

Fat Bud French Lavender
Lavandula x intermedia 'Grosso'

Honey Bush
Melianthus major

Aromatherapy can happen right at home. Inhale the scent of lavender
or jasmine and any stress you have will immediately begin to fall away.

CALIFORNIA STYLE, COAST TO COAST

Over the last twenty years, I have observed a positive groundswell in people's attitudes toward living outdoors. It is not an organized movement but a cultural zeitgeist, a shift in thinking about our relationship to the outdoor spaces we make and inhabit. People are now creating environments that are deeply personal and reflect their beliefs, values, hopes, and desires.

Having grown up in Santa Monica, it would be easy to think that this is a uniquely Californian mind-set. Southern California has historically been a hub of activity for modern outdoor living since the mid-twentieth century. It had the perfect ingredients for realizing the dream of outdoor living: great weather, lots of available open space, and a continual influx of new residents ready and willing to pursue that goal. As that trend has continued into the twenty-first century, I've come to realize that this attitude is not limited to a small section of the West Coast. It flourishes all over the country, from rooftops and terraces to beachfronts and forested areas, and, of course, in urban yards nationwide.

My first client in New York hired me because she wanted a "California-style garden." I took that to mean a dynamic and beautiful outdoor space that could really be lived in, which is exactly what she and her family now do. I have been to parties there in spring and summer and heard stories of Halloween celebrations, snowmen, and all kinds of events and activities held throughout the year in their compact outdoor space. The art of outdoor living can be practiced anywhere.

So when I travel to other parts of the country and encounter the same attitude toward outdoor living, I feel right at home. California is a state of mind. I take inspiration from seeing what people have done in all kinds of climates and environments. I find it endlessly fascinating to see how different people's imaginations have sparked their creativity and been put into play. I appreciate both the quiet peace of a wooded property enhanced by the subtle design of a thoughtful garden and the pop of a brightly colored poolside hangout that shouts out "join the fun!" Add a casual approach to entertaining and plenty of good food, drink, and conversation to the mix, and you have what I consider California living at its finest.

The cool blue waters of pool and ocean are a seamless match. The modernist-inspired pergola provides shade on hot summer days, as well as the structure for a fun hanging chair.

The insouciant poolside lounge at Jonathan Adler and Simon Doonan's weekend house embodies the dream of sunny California. Their built-in sectional is topped with a happy mix of colorful pillows and a custom ceramic wall piece, all envisioned in-house by the dynamic duo of design.

top left: A tabletop setting features one of the many Adler ceramic pieces that decorate the entire house. A small horse planter filled with succulents makes a no-fuss centerpiece that lasts for months. The bright colors and patterns used throughout pop wonderfully against the dark charcoal walls of the house.

top right: Jonathan tests out a myriad of new products at home, like these planters I covet. One gorgeous, full plant in a striking pot provides plenty of drama and eye candy.

right: Resident pooch Liberace has the right idea: a post-lunch nap. A cluster of outdoor chairs around a steel fire pit with sand underfoot makes a great casual spot for conversation, day and night.

opposite: The surprise of a wall tiled from top to bottom is one of many sumptuous touches throughout the house. Think of tile as outdoor wallpaper—the possibilities are endless.

above: The morning sun is best enjoyed in a cozy nook at the front of the house. If things get too bright, a roll-down shade fixes the problem; if things are too dark, a moon-like white globe can be flipped on for soft illumination.

opposite: The front courtyard entrance is the first room of the house. In the landscape designed by Vickie Cardaro, a Japanese maple flourishes as the centerpiece and chunky stepping stones, set in a field of crushed shells, create an informal and beachy pathway.

above: A mixed flock of chickens, ducks, and geese greet owners and guests at the cobalt gate of Once in a Blue Moon Farm. Statuesque hollyhocks (*Alcea rosea*) pop up along the path leading to the coops, where freshly laid eggs are gathered daily.

left: The pop of color from the red petal-like chairs, contrasting with the purple and chartreuse foliage, mimics the cheery flowers in Nancy Heckler's delightful garden in the state of Washington.

top left: A former Angeleno, Shana Lloyd traded in her city life when she fell in love with her home and farm on Orcas Island off the coast of Washington. Teaming up with daughter Sarah and son Zachary, their abundant orchards are full of some of the island's oldest fruit trees, and produce tons of apples, quinces, plums, and pears.

top right: Freshly cut homegrown flowers are casually arranged and placed throughout the property at Once in a Blue Moon Farm. This simple arrangement of blue hibiscus, yarrow, and fragrant fennel provides many days of pleasure.

right: Nancy Heckler's sumptuous vegetable garden beautifully intermingles flowers with edibles. Big drifts of Swiss chard are planted both as an adored ornamental and a food crop that is easy to harvest and delicious to eat.

EXTENDING THE SEASON

Not all of us live in warm and temperate climates, but there are things we can all do to extend our warm seasons and increase our engagement with our gardens. Here are some suggestions to prolong your outdoor time.

INCLUDE A FIRE PIT In addition to creating a compelling focal point, the warmth of a fire pit will inspire the use of your garden at night and during cooler weather.

PLANT FOR ALL SEASONS Combine evergreen perennials for year-round structure and annuals for seasonal interest and color in windowboxes, pots, and planters.

PLANT BULBS In cooler climates, bulbs bring a welcome burst of color in winter and spring and offer a taste of what's to come in summer.

GROW INSIDE Herbs and citrus can be grown indoors, as long as they get some sunlight.

CREATE AN ARRANGEMENT I often use a succulent or air plant (also known as epiphyte) in a low bowl or small planter to brighten a tabletop.

GRILL ALL YEAR Cooking outside is possible in just about any season—don't let damp or cold weather stop you.

BUILD A COVERED PATIO A sheltered space will keep you cool in the summer and warm in the winter.

ADD HEAT Choose from a range of freestanding and wall-mounted heaters, or install radiant heat for warmth in cool climates.

GROW WINTER CROPS In fall and winter in more temperate climates, plant greens, root vegetables, and herbs in your edible garden for year-round production.

PREPARE FOR SPRING During the winter, start thinking about what plants you want to add, mulch beds, cut back perennials as needed, and sow seeds in tiny containers indoors to get a jump on the warmer months.

In Wainscott, New York, interior designer Eric Hughes works his magic in putting together a chic outdoor seating area. The space is complete with a poured-concrete fireplace, and invites hours of hanging out for many months of the year.

top left: In this trio of gardens by Austin landscape designer Mark Word, corten steel planters and crunchy gravel feel right at home. This handsome composition uses only a handful of plants but achieves great results.

top right: A stunning red Japanese maple holds center court. The layering of warm plants and furniture is a lovely touch in this intimate seating area.

left: A simple water feature flanked by multi-trunked trees artfully frames the greater landscape.

opposite: At Jardineros, Word's nursery, the thoughtfully composed grouping of plants inspires ideas for future gardens and the spectacular pink wall creates a stunning backdrop for the vivid shades of green foliage.

top left: A wooded property on the East Coast inspires vacations at home. A cotton hammock strung between two trees is the perfect spot for reading, relaxing, and the occasional nap—a light touch at the home of interior designer Suzanne Shaker.

top right: Shaker's modern aesthetic beautifully complements the work of architect Cary Tamarkin, a frequent collaborator. A painted black pergola with modernist spider legs shelters a pair of low-slung chairs in upstate New York.

left: The two teamed up again on a beachfront property on Shelter Island. A generous wood deck and pergola artfully extend the house into the landscape.

opposite: An outdoor shower is seamlessly knit into the woodwork of the house exterior. A low, railing-height wall frames the view and provides screening.

left: A sumptuous pool in New Orleans literally embraces nature with a lushly planted perimeter. Using plants pressed up against a pool is a beautiful and bold move that creates enormous impact and romance.

above: Rough-hewn stones are exquisitely laid to form inviting stairs and chunky garden walls. The landscape design firm Mosaic Gardens in Eugene, Oregon, created this richly layered composition of brilliant foliage and flowers.

A tile backsplash mirrors the vivid green foliage in the super-chic Manhattan apartment of architect David Mann. Like a Fabergé egg, small and exquisite, David has crafted a divine experience of outdoor living, enjoyed from inside and out.

top: David transformed a long, narrow terrace into a lush garden oasis with an abundance of terra-cotta pots and verdant plantings. The transparent quality of vintage Sculptura chairs helps maintain an open sense of space.

bottom: The end facing the neighbors is made beautiful and private with tall, leafy screening, whereas the opposite end of the terrace is kept open to enjoy the city view. Softly clipped topiary cones add some welcome structure against the brick walls of the building.

above: A small rooftop terrace doubles as a place of work and relaxation. With no native soil available, custom fiberglass planters were filled to the brim to create a private and colorful garden in the sky.

right: Working in different climates is a wonderful challenge that I relish. The flat backyard on the ground floor of an updated brownstone was reimagined as a bi-level patio with a built-in dining area. Our client wanted a California-style garden, which I interpreted as a lush, private space for family activities, grilling, and entertaining.

Plum Pudding Coral Bells
Heuchera 'Plum Pudding'

Evergreen Miscanthus
Miscanthus transmorrisonensis

Crested Ligularia
Farfugium japonicum 'Cristata'

Yellow Twig Dogwood
Cornus sericea 'Flaviramea'

Blue Glow Agave
Agave 'Blue Glow'

Southern Splendor Dracaena Palm
Cordyline 'Southern Splendor'

Plants with Year-round Interest

Berkeley Purple Flax
Phormium 'Wildwood'

Compact Bronze Hinoki Cypress
Chamaecyparis obtusa 'Pygmaea Aurescens'

Cynthia Giddy Aloe
Aloe 'Cynthia Giddy'

Vanderwolf's Pyramid Limber Pine
Pinus flexilis 'Vanderwolf's Pyramid'

Dragon's Blood Stonecrop
Sedum spurium 'Dragon's Blood'

Coral Bark Japanese Maple
Acer palmatum 'Sango-kaku'

To guarantee that your garden never has a dull moment, try plants
with vibrant foliage colors, varied textures, and striking silhouettes.

RESOURCES

POTS & PLANTERS

Bauer Pottery
bauerpottery.com

Vessel USA Inc.
architecturalpottery.com

Potted
pottedstore.com

Jackalope
jackalope.com

Greenform
green-form.com

West Elm
westelm.com

Sprout Home
sprouthome.com

GROWERS

Monrovia
monrovia.com

California Cactus Center
cactuscenter.com

Annie's Annuals
anniesannuals.com

White Flower Farm
whiteflowerfarm.com

Geraniaceae
geraniaceae.com

Bamboo Headquarters
bamboohq.com

Avant Gardens
avantgardensne.com

Companion Plants
companionplants.com

Santa Rosa Gardens
santarosagardens.com

Gardens of the Blue Ridge
gardensoftheblueridge.com

Mountain Valley Growers
mountainvalleygrowers.com

Logee's Plants for Home & Garden
logees.com

Plant Delights Nursery
plantdelights.com

Four Winds Growers
fourwindsgrowers.com

Cacti.com
cacti.com

Australian Native Plants Nursery
australiaplants.com

Stokes Tropicals
stokestropicals.plants.com

Edible Landscaping
ediblelandscaping.com

OUTDOOR FURNITURE & ACCESSORIES

Plain Air
plainair.com

Jonathan Adler
jonathanadler.com

Stan Bitters
ten10site.com

Fermob
fermobusa.com

Circa50, Inc.
circa50.com

Design Within Reach
dwr.com

Casamidy
casamidy.com

Maison Midi
maison-midi.com

Mecox
mecox.com

OK
okthestore.com

Mosaik
e-mosaik.com

ReForm School
reformschoolrules.com

JANUS et Cie*
janusetcie.com

Henry Hall Designs*
henryhalldesigns.com

Ilan Dei Venice
ilandeivenice.com

Cap Sud*
capsudusa.com

OUTDOOR FABRICS

Perennials*
perennialsfabrics.com

Les Toiles Du Soleil
lestoilesdusoleilnyc.com

Sunbrella*
sunbrella.com

Kravet*
kravet.com

Holly Hunt*
hollyhunt.com

Duralee*
duralee.com

Trina Turk*
fschumacher.com/collections/trinaturk.aspx

FIRE PITS & FIREPLACES

Plain Air
plainair.com

Potted
pottedstore.com

Design Within Reach
dwr.com

Modfire
modfire.com

EcoSmart Fire
ecosmartfire.com

Colombo Construction Corp
firefeatures.com

COOKING EQUIPMENT

Lynx
lynxgrills.com

Weber
weber.com

Primo Grills and Smokers
primogrill.com

Earthstone
earthstoneovens.com

OUTDOOR RUGS & MATS

Plastica
plasticashop.com

Dash & Albert Rug Company
dashandalbert.com

Chilewich
chilewich.com

SEEDS

Renee's Garden
reneesgarden.com

Seeds of Change
seedsofchange.com

Seed Savers Exchange
seedsavers.org

The Cook's Garden
cooksgarden.com

GARDEN SHOPS

Rolling Greens
rollinggreensnursery.com

Inner Gardens
innergardens.com

The Gardener
thegardener.com

Mecox
mecox.com

Terrain
shopterrain.com

SPECIALTY NURSERIES

Jardineros
jardinerosnursery.com

Flora Grubb Gardens
floragrubb.com

ORGANIC GARDEN SUPPLIES

Peaceful Valley
groworganic.com

Dr. Earth
drearth.net

BEEKEEPING

Backwards Beekeepers
backwardsbeekeepers.com

STONE, GRAVEL, & PEBBLES

Bourget Bros.
bourgetbros.com

Malibu Stone
malibustone.com

American Soil & Stone
americansoil.com

TILE

Mission Tile West
missiontilewest.com

Daltile
daltile.com

Granada Tile
granadatile.com

Heath Ceramics
heathceramics.com

Mosaic House
mosaichse.com

Kismet Tile
kismettile.com

Ann Sacks
annsacks.com

COMMUNITY RESOURCES

The Edible Schoolyard Project
edibleschoolyard.org

Garden School Foundation
gardenschoolfoundation.org

American Community
Gardening Association
communitygarden.org

BOOKS

Sunset Western Garden Book
Editors of Sunset Magazine

Gardens Are For People
by Thomas D. Church

*Garrett Eckbo:
Modern Landscapes for Living*
by Marc Treib

*Tomorrow's Garden:
Design and Inspiration for a New Age
of Sustainable Gardening*
by Stephen Orr

The Edible Front Yard
by Ivette Soler

Edible Schoolyard: A Universal Idea
by Alice Waters

*The 50 Mile Bouquet:
Seasonal, Local and Sustainable Flowers*
by Debra Prinzing

The Complete Idiot's Guide to Beekeeping
by Dean Stiglitz and Laurie Herboldsheimer

Italian Grill
by Mario Batali with Judith Sutton

Designing with Plants
by Piet Oudolf with Noël Kingsbury

*The Collector's Garden:
Designing with Extraordinary Plants*
by Ken Druse

*These great trade resources are available only through
a design professional.

221

First published in the United States of America in 2014
by Rizzoli International Publications, Inc.
300 Park Avenue South
New York, NY 10010
www.rizzoliusa.com

© 2014 Judy Kameon

Principal photography by Erik Otsea

Illustrations by Judy Kameon

Chapter number compositions by Judy Kameon and Erik Otsea

2014 2015 2016 2017 / 10 9 8 7 6 5 4 3 2 1

Distributed in the U.S. trade by Random House, New York

Printed in China

Design by Glen Nakasako, SMOG Design, Inc.

ISBN-13: 978-0-8478-4219-3

Library of Congress Control Number: 2013950262

ACKNOWLEDGMENTS

Making this book has been an epic journey, and one that I could not have made alone. I am deeply humbled by the generosity and support of the many people who have been involved along the way. In particular, I would like to offer thanks to the following:

Barbara Farmer, my eternal gratitude. You are my trusted right hand and left brain, who wrangled this book into shape with pom-poms on one hip and a whip on the other. I am in your debt.

Christopher Steighner, my kind and intelligent editor, who consistently offered guidance, ideas, and reassurance with patience and grace.

Carla Glasser, my agent, who nurtured this book into existence, much to my delight.

Our brilliant book designers, Jeri Heiden and Glen Nakasako of SMOG Design, Inc. Your magnificent transformation of masses of writing, photos, and illustrations into a gorgeous book was a thrill I will never forget.

Jonathan Adler for his fabulous foreword, gobs of style, and a decade of cherished friendship.

The many talented photographers who have contributed to this project, and whose gorgeous images allow us to share what we do for so few with so many.

The myriad of friends, artists, and fellow designers who generously opened their doors and shared their inspiring work with us all.

My beloved sounding boards—Jon Huck, Dana Bauer, Stephen Orr, Lindsey Taylor, Richard Friedman, Alisa Tager, Stephanie Emerson, Shannon Shelly, and Caitlin Scanlon—for their continual support and encouragement.

The wonderful clients who are the patrons of our practice—thank you for the opportunity to make the world a more beautiful place, a little bit at a time.

The team at Elysian Landscapes and Plain Air, past and present, who work tirelessly to make our designs come to life and keep things running—Barbara Farmer, David Ellien, Natalia Saucedo, Dana Bauer, Katy Valentin, Teresa Bruner, Matthew Kendall, Michael Kirchmann Jr., and Ivette Soler.

The masterful builder Tim Foster and his fantastic crew, for realizing our designs and dreams through the years. Words cannot express my appreciation.

My mother, Ruthie, for introducing me to a life full of gardens, cooking, entertaining, and travel—and the deeply held belief that I should always do what I love.

My late father, Herb, for passing along his exacting attention to detail, drive, and passion for art, architecture, and good food—not necessarily in that order.

Our son, Ian, for being a great sport on countless photo shoots and a shining example of someone who finds joy in life outside.

And most of all—the man behind the camera, my partner and husband, Erik Otsea, who was relentless in his pursuit for the best photographs possible. I could not have done this without you.

—Judy Kameon